trust
redefined

learning to surrender through
the journey of unknowns

RACHEL WILLIAMS
with forward by Curt Hinkle, Ed.D

To contact Rachel for speaking or questions:
rachel@neversobroken.com

———————— • • ————————

Printed in the United States of America
First Printing, 2019
ISBN 978-1-7332591-0-1

Never So Broken
P.O. Box 1267
Eau Claire, WI 54702
www.NeverSoBroken.com

Interior and cover design by
Jodi Stevens Design
www.jodistevensdesign.com

This book is dedicated to my mom,
who has always challenged me to face myself,
even when I haven't wanted to.

Contents

Forward

BY CURT HINKLE, Ed.D

Rachel Williams did not set out to write another book, she certainly had no plans to write *this* book. She sensed God's urging and started writing. What follows this forward is a result of her obedience to His prompting – *Trust Redefined: Learning to Surrender through the Journey of Unknowns*.

As Rachel's dad, I have watched her story unfold in real-life. As she wrote this book, I was privileged to walk with her through the writing process and help her clarify her thoughts in a manner that honored God, her journey, and her potential readers. Her journey in writing this began with raw honesty, a refreshing trait that she carries throughout the book.

I once asked her what her hopes were as she wrote *Trust Redefined*. Her response was:

My hope is that women of all stages of life feel better equipped and encouraged to use God's Word, and trust in God's faithfulness even when feelings and circumstances are less than ideal. I want to show women how completely alive and applicable God's Word is. I hope they will feel inspired to grow in their knowledge of the Bible and desire to apply it to their lives. My hope is that women feel a camaraderie in human feelings and "failings" in faith. That they know they're not alone in what they experience, and that it is possible to "get it all wrong", and STILL be strengthened, challenged, and used by God.

Her hopes have come to fruition before my own eyes. Rachel does a wonderful job of telling her story in a manner that will draw you in and, at the same time, create a desire to better know and follow Jesus. The operative word throughout the book is *trust*. We either trust God or we don't. The key to trusting God is our definition of trust. As her story unfolds, Rachel moves from a definition of trust that is self-focused to one based on the understanding that God has our best interests in mind. As you read through the journey that took place for this to happen, you might also find a new definition of trust.

Gratitude is another operative word that runs throughout *Trust Redefined*. Brennan Manning, in his book *Ruthless Trust*, suggests that one could say that they trust God, but without an abiding spirit of gratitude, the words may be hollow. Because of the sense of gratitude that permeates Rachel's story, the words that follow are far from hollow. Her deep gratitude for the way God redefined her trust in Him through His Word is evident throughout the unfolding of her story.

The presence of scripture, God's Word for living, is core to Rachel's story. As I read the manuscript, I kept thinking, "She spent a lot of time drawing on scripture, making sure she had the exact right passages." As a practical theologian, in a world filled with hollow opinions, I find this use of scripture refreshing. As you read, you will realize that she didn't seek to find scripture to support her suppositions; rather it will become evident that it was her consistent reliance on scripture throughout her journey that led to a *Trust Redefined*.

So, enjoy! I sure did. Oh, and be ready for transformation! Throughout *Trust Redefined*, Rachel provides a number of questions to consider as you journey through the book. *Take the time to ponder them.* Emerging from such pondering might be the life you've always hoped for.

Curt Hinkle, Ed.D.

Introduction

WHY AM I DOING THIS?

Blinking cursor on the screen, I find myself staring at my computer, unmoving and saying aloud, "Lord, why am I doing this?" It's 11 degrees outside, there is no sun in the sky, my kids are at school, the baby is sleeping, my curtains are drawn, my phone is playing worship music, my Bible is strewn out on my bed, and I feel completely consumed with darkness. I have felt it encompassing me since the *moment* our first women's conference ended.

I am a co-founder of a brand new women's ministry in our community. On a prayer and a Bible verse we embarked on putting together a women's conference. We prayed for 50 women to sign up and we had almost 300 in attendance. In fact, we sold out 3 months in advance. The conference was amazing, lives were impacted — *changed*! I walked around the entire weekend on such a spiritual high. The Holy Spirit was there, Jesus was there! We prayed He would bring it, and HE DID!

And yet as the last woman left the building, I turned a physical corner in the venue and felt myself slam spiritually into a wall. It has been years since I have felt such complete and utter darkness envelope me. Fear creeps in to remind me, *The last time almost ended my life.*

So here I sit feeling utterly consumed by this darkness. Like a heavy blanket I didn't ask for, it is suffocating me, immersing me, and engulfing me in pelting lies that seem to come at me like rapid fire every minute of the day.

Staring at this computer screen, feeling overwhelmingly compelled by the Holy Spirit to start typing, I am asking God what good could possibly come from beginning to write in such a poor mental state. *What could I possibly have to share?* "You don't", He whispers to my soul, "My Word will be your guide."

I admit, I don't want to be typing. I have no idea how this will end. I have no idea what will end up strewn across these pages. What I know is that I feel a pull from the Holy Spirit to start. And as I use the pages of Scripture — God's Word — to fight my way out of my own personal darkness, as I let God fight the battle for me, as I rest in HIS promises for me, I am going to bring you along on the journey with me, in obedience to the call I feel pressed on my heart. I know I am far from the only one who has experienced this kind of darkness. I think we could all benefit from hearing what the Bible says about fighting our way out of such a time.

Perhaps some are thinking they don't even know what I am talking about when I say darkness: *Does she mean depression? Sadness?*

This darkness I speak of is a place where I simply feel an absence of light in my life and in my soul. Not because Jesus has left me, but based on my spiritual or physical circumstances, I feel Satan — the very enemy of God — begging me to throw in the towel on trusting God almighty. Satan is beckoning me to admit defeat, abandon my belief that God is good, and that He has my best interest in mind. The enemy is seducing me with the lie that I can make it through this on my own. So I find myself at a fork in the road where I must decide which path my feet will follow: believe his lies or stand on the solid ground of God's truth alone.

If you find yourself standing in darkness as well, yours might exist for a different reason. You might be walking through a vastly different type of darkness than me. Or perhaps you are reading this and life actually feels pretty great for you right now, so you wonder how this could apply to you? Unfortunately seasons of darkness are a part of following Jesus, and we can never predict when Satan will set his sights on us trying to take us down. This darkness I speak of threatens to undo all the good we have in our lives, the ways we've grown in our faith, and the very joy God has promised us when we walk by His spirit.

Darkness wants us to believe that God is not trustworthy and that we have only ourselves to rely on.

"This is the message we have heard from Him and proclaim to you, that God is light, and in Him is no darkness at all." (1 John 1:5)

Ladies, here is the thing: **Darkness. Is. Not. From. The. LORD!** When we feel consumed by it, we can KNOW with certainty that we are not meant to stay in it. There is NO darkness in God *at all*.

So how do we fight it? What can remove these feelings of despair from our minds? The pelting lies in our thoughts?

Introduction

I will tell you this, it will not be on our own! I will never fight this darkness and successfully win on my own. Trust me I have tried — oh boy have I tried. *But I am not enough to overcome it.*

Harsh as it may be, you are not enough to simply pluck yourself out of a dark season and go on your merry way. I am not enough to create a lasting change in my life. There might be some who question that, who think they can fake it till they make it. And there is some validity to that mindset, but will it ever completely give you victory? Has it ever *completely* freed you?

It hasn't for me.

And I doubt it has for you.

It's God's Word that gives freedom. Psalm 119:130 says, *"The unfolding of your words gives light; it imparts understanding to the simple."*

It imparts understanding to the simple.

That is me. *The simple.*

I am not a scholar, I am a stay-at-home mom who has a bunch of kids (a bunch!). As a woman who is in a season of desperately seeking light, I am going to go with God's Word on this. I am going to trust that there will be freedom for me, light in the end of this, *"For it is you [God] who lights my lamp; the Lord my God lightens my darkness."* (Psalm 18:28)

As I sit in my darkness, I am fighting it. God will deliver me, and I am proclaiming victory before this even begins. When Jesus went to the cross for you, for me, He took on sin. He took on death, and when He came back to life, He defeated what Satan intended to ruin for *the entire human race* in the garden of Eden. If Jesus can free the entire human race from something the enemy meant to result in our eternal death, I can rest assured Jesus will win this battle for me. And He will win your battle for you.

Chapter One
WHY IS IT SO DARK IN HERE?

I find myself picturing what kind of woman is holding this book in her hands right now, reading these words. Who are you? What caused you to pick it up, borrow it, or purchase it? Are you sitting in your own place of darkness? Is there something causing you to seek light? Is there something threatening to unravel your trust in God?

As I mentioned, my darkness happened overnight — *this time.* I believe it is 100% spiritual warfare — *this time.* I am in a season where God is using me with the gifts He has given me, and women are seeing Jesus as a result. Women are being challenged in their faith and equipped to use their God-given gifts to further His kingdom. Satan hates that and he will stop at nothing to take me down.

Stop the girl, stop God.

Or so he thinks.

I will never understand how the enemy works. Why won't he admit defeat? Does he not have access to God's Word like we do? The apostle John says that Jesus was with God in the beginning, He was a part of everything that was made, and in Him is the light of mankind. He goes on to say in John 1:5 that, *"The light shines in the darkness, and the darkness has not overcome it."* **Jesus cannot be overcome by the darkness.** He has already won the war, He too has faced the darkness, and He was *not overcome.*

If you're familiar with the book of Revelation, the ending of this physical world is already spelled out. Spoiler alert — God wins!

I wish Satan would just give up already. Wave the white flag. Be done with trying to take down those who love the Lord, and even those who are not sure where they land, but are in the process of seeking Him.

Leave. Us. Alone.

But he won't. Because he hates God *that much*. He will pour all of his efforts into plucking off as many as he can from joining the family of believers, until the *last possible moment*. He wants as many as he can get. If God intends to use me or you to bring in more brothers and sisters in Christ, we better count on the enemy aiming his best efforts directly at us.

Honestly, it's not a bad strategy.

I hate to give props to the bad guy, but the devil sure is onto something here. Sometimes what he has thrown at me in the past *has* deterred me. It *has* stopped me in my tracks. It *has* rerouted my plans. It *has* made me doubt my Creator.

But not this time! I am a girl who is using her Bible and trusting in God's ability to see me through. And I fully intend to bring you with me — claiming our victory together based on God's Word alone!

All throughout this book I'm going to list questions. I am going to write them in first person. I think it's more impactful when we ask ourselves questions than when we are asked them by another person. I really encourage you to take the time to ask yourself each of them, even if they're hard. Take time to write down your answer, I'll leave space for you.

In what ways have I let the enemy thwart what God has asked me to do in my life?

_____

_____

_____

_____

Maybe I don't recognize it as Satan, maybe it just feels hard and I want to give up. Is there truth of that in my life? What might be the evidence if so?

_____

_____

_____

_____

Perhaps I don't feel thwarted by the enemy, I simply feel an absence of light. What are some examples of a lack of joy in my life?

_____

_____

_____

_____

Thinking big picture, is God onto something in my life? How might He want to use my current circumstances to further His kingdom? To grow my faith? To encourage another Christian in his or her life?

_____

_____

_____

_____

If I walked away from what God is asking me to do, what might I miss out on? Who wins if I do?

_____

_____

_____

_____

➤ ⟋ l ⟍ ◄

So what brings you here? Are you like me, feeling an over looming shadow across your life? Have you had something difficult happen recently? Do you just feel unlike yourself these days? Or are you doing fantastic in your life, but you know that in your walk with Jesus you can expect dark seasons to come back in someday? Maybe you are just starting to realize — today with this book in hand — that something doesn't feel right.

Ask yourself these questions. Take a moment to let yourself sit in them for a little bit:

When is the last time I experienced what Rachel is describing as darkness (an absence of light, the struggle to believe that God is trustworthy)?

_____

_____

Is there a darkness I can feel in my life right now? If so, what is it?

_____

_____

_____

_____

What are my coping mechanisms when I don't feel like myself?

_____

_____

_____

_____

What things do I cling to when searching for fulfillment? Do I go to the Bible, prayer, and godly counsel? Or do I retreat to things like TV, the internet, and gossip?

_____

_____

_____

_____

Maybe you're here because you are grieving *someone*. Maybe you've lost a loved one you cannot imagine facing the days without. Maybe you've lost someone you didn't even get a chance to know (pregnancy/adoption loss). Maybe you're grieving the someone who hasn't arrived yet, you're waiting for God to bring you a spouse or a long awaited child.

Maybe you're here because you're grieving *something*. You lost that career that you loved, or your spouse lost the job that provided financial security. Maybe you lost a friendship that has left a gaping hole in your heart and life. Perhaps you recently moved and you just feel lost, nothing feels familiar, and you wonder if you will ever find your place.

It is possible that your church has hurt you, and you don't feel safe anymore among the body of believers. You find yourself wondering who can you trust, or even worse, if you will ever be able to trust again.

Maybe you're experiencing something like my current season, maybe the darkness is just trying to take you down. Maybe it's completely spiritual, and circumstances don't even align with it — life is fine, you just feel the darkness.

Are you walking through postpartum depression? Post adoption depression?

I've been there. Twice. You feel like you should be completely overjoyed to have been given such a beautiful blessing and yet, things feel anything but happy. The thoughts are dark, the workload feels heavy, and you just want to crawl back into your bed, if you are even getting out of it.

Did you know premenopausal and postmenopausal are real things women struggle with? Perhaps this is you and you feel completely thrown for a loop by the unexpected internal chaos of your season.

Maybe you're here because you want to grow in your faith and learn to trust God more. Maybe you're here proactively for the unknown seasons that we can trust are to come. Perhaps you feel this book will help you encourage someone around you?

Whatever it is, I pray this book is good news to you. I hope the scriptures on these pages, the stories I share, and the questions I ask challenge you to dig in deeper on your reliance in Jesus.

As I experience — for the umpteenth time — this looming shadow over my life, I believe I am supposed to share with you the different seasons I have walked through darkness in the past. First I need to paint a picture of who I am, so you can see how deeply the seasons have altered me.

I am a really bubbly person. Outgoing for sure. I love people. In fact, until I had 8 kids, people didn't ever exhaust me, they seemed to give me life! I love big crowds, and large family gatherings. I love to host and I love to be in the center of it all. Not for the attention, but because that's where all the fun is! I tend to see the positive in most circumstances, or at least I can view things for what they really are; rarely am I a negative person. I love to laugh, I am often described by people as someone who loves humor and loves to make other people laugh! I bring laughter into all of my conversations, as long as it's appropriate, and sometimes maybe even when it isn't — oops!

I have a lot of energy. All of my life people have marveled at how much I accomplish, sometimes without any caffeine! I have been told I exuberate energy everywhere I go, and I rile people up! I get people excited about what is to come. I am a passionate person and I love to inspire others in those passions.

These descriptions are not who I have decided to be, they are simply who God created me to be. I don't have to work to be this person, it is who I am naturally. Just read any of my personality tests, this completely and accurately describes me.

I am a naturally positive person. I don't have to work hard to be happy. Life just feels good to me. On top of that, I am a generally pretty thankful person. Years ago I worked at a coffee shop. Whoever worked the shift together would split the tips at the end. After I worked there a few months I found out people loved to work with me because I was so bubbly and personable that the customers seemed to tip the best when I was working! People were actually trading shifts to try and work with me. I had no idea, it's just who I am, I absolutely love to converse with people and find out about their lives.

This is my personality, even without Jesus, this is how I live my life.

Until I am facing the darkness.

When I feel darkness creep in, it is like a switch is suddenly flipped and a completely different Rachel exists. Inside for sure, and the people closest to me can completely see the change on the outside. I begin to see life through a different lens: everything feels sour, everything is a burden, everything robs me of joy — I don't want to fight anymore. At one point in my life I even rolled over and told the enemy to *just have me*, I didn't want to fight anymore because it just didn't seem worth it.

For that time, nothing seemed worth it. Not my husband. Not my family. Not my children.

Except *maybe* my Savior. But He only felt worth it in that moment if He was willing to fight for me. Because at that time in my life, I no longer seemed to have it in me to fight.

That was a *really* bad time. But we will get to that a bit later.

Do me a favor, dig into these questions for a bit before we move on. Feel free to grab a notebook and take some notes if you don't want to use the pages here, but write them somewhere! It is so important when we are hoping for a change in our hearts to truly let God work through our minds as we process. If we simply glance over questions, it is unlikely much will stick or lead to lasting change. However, often when we start writing, doors begin to open in our heart and we can feel God begin to reveal things through that simple act that we might otherwise have been quick to miss.

What are some indicators that I am on the verge of surrendering to the darkness?

_____

_____

_____

_____

_____

_____

_____

_____

Have I already waved the white flag? If so, why?

_____

_____

_____

_____

_____

_____

_____

If not, what's keeping me from giving up?

_____

_____

_____

_____

_____

_____

_____

Chapter Two

WHY ARE MY LIGHTS TURNED OFF?!

We often want answers. Actually in life, it's pretty much safe to say we always want answers. *Why did that person I love have to die? What is keeping my husband from loving me like I need? Why can't I get pregnant? When are things going to get easier? Why does everyone else seem to have more money than me? Why? Why? Why? Why? Why?*

I cannot give you answers, as much as I'd like to, but I know I find myself asking the same questions when I walk through hard seasons. I'm asking myself questions even now. *Why do this amazingly big thing for You Lord, witness to all these women, do what I believe you asked me to, only to be slammed with spiritual attack when it is done?*

Why God?

Paul tells us in 1 Corinthians 2:11 (NLT), *"No one can know a person's thoughts except that person's own spirit, and no one can know God's thoughts except God's own Spirit."*

In other words: God is God, and only He gets to know the answers we are often searching for: when, where, why?

UGH.

What. a. buzz. kill.

I mean *no offense* to God's Word, but when I want answers, the last thing I want to be told is, "just trust me."

Does anyone else feel that way?

If God alone knows the answers, does that then mean that this thing I am walking through — this thing you are walking through — comes as *no surprise* to Him?

If you are like me, you might get things mixed up, somehow believing that God is not entirely in the know. Does it ever feel like maybe He is not paying attention — like something happened to us when He "wasn't looking"?

Does it feel like what we are experiencing is somehow a surprise to Him?

Does this confuse you? Upset you even? If so, that is alright. It is okay to bring our confusion and disappointment to God. He will meet us where we are and if we ask for it, He will bring within us a change of heart — a correction in our thinking.

Here's the thing friends, we can rest assured that **He knows!** He is NOT on the outskirts of our lives, He is not watching from afar, He is not one ounce surprised!

I would love to share with you all of Psalm 139, but it's pretty long, so I won't put it on these pages in its entirety, however if you find yourself thinking *He must not really know*, I highly encourage you to read all 24 verses of it.

I hope the portions I share below with you will make you thirsty for more; I broke it down line by line. I challenge you to pause after each line, don't just brush through it like we often do — drink it in! Stop and ask yourself after each line — "Do I believe this is true?"

> *Lord, You have examined me and know all about me.*
> (Do I believe this is true?)
>
> *You know when I sit down and when I get up.*
> (Do I believe this is true?)
>
> *You know my thoughts before I think them.*
> (Do I believe this is true?)
>
> *You know where I go and where I lie down.*
> (Do I believe this is true?)
>
> *You know everything I do.*
> (Do I believe this is true?)
>
> *Lord, even before I say a word, you already know it.*
> (Do I believe this is true?)
>
> *You are all around me—in front and in back—and have put Your hand on me.* (Do I believe this is true?)
>
> *Your knowledge is amazing to me; it is more than I can understand.* (Do I believe this is true?)
>
> (Psalm 139:1-6 NCV)

I just want to keep going, it's beautiful!

We think we know those around us: our children, our husbands, our best friends, our sisters. Heck, we think we know ourselves! But there is no one in this world who can possibly know us like our God, *not even ourselves*. He knows what will come out of our mouths before we even say it!

Lord have mercy, does that make anyone panic a bit?

I admit I don't always know what is going to come out when I open my mouth half the time! Of course this isn't entirely an awesome character trait, but He knows before even we do! I already admitted to you that I have no idea what's going to be in this book, I'm just typing as I go and trusting God to lead.

But HE KNOWS.

My friends, He. is. in. it. with. us!

Whatever I am experiencing, *whatever* you are walking through, *He knows*. He knew before it even began. He is intimately acquainted with the times we get up, the places we go, even the number of hairs on our head (Matthew 10:30)!

There is no darkness in our lives, in our minds, or in our hearts that *He did not see coming*.

Have I been believing that my dark seasons come as a surprise to God?

_____

_____

_____

_____

In what ways do I feel like He isn't paying attention to my life?

_____

_____

_____

_____

Which parts of Psalm 139 were the hardest for me to believe?

_____

_____

_____

_____

Am I willing to trust God that He knows what is to happen and when it is to happen? Why or why not?

_____

_____

_____

_____

➤⟩⟨◅

I'm scratching my head as I'm typing, asking — *what am I even saying here? I don't exactly like where this is heading Lord!*

God are you behind everything that is happening to us?

Are you okay with it all?

What exactly is God's role in what I am walking through, or in what you are walking through?

Jesus tells us in John 16:33 (NIV), *"In this world you will have trouble."*

If we believe that the Bible is true, that Jesus never sinned — therefore never lied — we are left with the only option of believing that statement as truth. I'm going to go so far as to call it a *promise*.

GULP. "In this world you will have trouble."

Not exactly the kind of promise we usually like to cling to in our faith is it? Certainly not the one I jump to when I need encouragement.

He tells us we will have trouble. *He prepares us for it.* He says it because He already knows what is to come. Hmm, doesn't that sound like 1 Corinthians 2:11 again? (*No one can know God's thoughts except God's own Spirit...*)

Following Jesus doesn't mean we are signing up for a life of luxury, or a free pass from pain. I mean technically that will come, but not until we leave this earth. On this side of Heaven, *we will have troubles.*

I'm not personally a fan of this part. It's like when we are signing up for marriage: we really just want the fun, the good times, the health. We don't want the sickness and the bad times. Certainly not the "until death do us part." I think this happens in our faith. We want the peace and joy that Jesus offers, but we don't want the trouble. Sometimes when tough things come, we simply bow out.

This is just too hard.

God's servant, Joseph, reminds us that God uses intended evil for eventual good (Genesis 50:20).

But here's the kicker, *we have to stick it out.*

What are some warnings that I might be in a season where I'm tempted to bow out?

_____

_____

On a scale of 1-10, how ready am I to toss my hands up and say, "enough"?

Maybe you aren't ready to give up. Maybe you're in this to the end, believing in what God promises in His Word when He says, *"The people dwelling in darkness have seen a great light, and for those dwelling in the region and shadow of death, on them a light has dawned."* (Matthew 4:16)

Our responses to dark times are going to be different from one another. Heck, mine has been different from season to season! Sometimes I can't even fully grasp how I responded to a dark season until years later when reflecting on it in retrospect.

The first time I walked through a dark season was marked by years of infertility, adoption scams, and losses. Every time Joey and I turned a corner it felt like we were being kicked down. My response was to "believe." If I read my old blog, it's lined with words of complete faith in God, trusting that He had a plan for us, and it would appear that my faith was strong and growing through that season.

In fact, until the writing of this very book, that is exactly how I would have described that season in my life. I often say I am even thankful for it, because of how much it did for my faith. It was my faith that I clung to, it was my faith that got me through.

But if I'm honest with myself — and you — about that season in my life, I am realizing only now, over a decade later, that I really just "believed" in getting what I wanted in the end. I believed God would give me a baby. Not because of some spiritual vision God gave me, that I decided to stake my claim in. No, my belief was nowhere near rooted in God being good, God being in control, or God being *enough*.

Being completely honest and retrospective, I can admit that God was not enough for me at that time. I wanted a baby, and that is the only ending I was okay with.

I wouldn't have settled for *no*. I wouldn't have settled for a life that banked on 2 Corinthians 12:19 where God promises that His grace is sufficient for me.

My response to a dark season seemed at the time to be "renewed faith". But now I can see it was really just a renewed faith in *what I wanted*.

That is what I fought for. Not God's promises, not His ultimate authority over my life, not trusting against all heartache. No, I was fighting *for what I wanted*.

Marshall Segal wrote for desiringgod.org, "*You have traded the truth about God for images of the truth, manufactured by your own mind. You've loved what you've learned about God more than God himself.*"

This was how I lived life through my first dark season. I created an idea in my head about a faithful God who would produce for me what I wanted, *if I believed enough*. Not because of who He was, but because of what I wanted.

That is a false theology.

That is a false god.

I will not sugar coat it my friends. If your faith resembles this, you have created an idol out of a false god.

"*They exchanged the truth about God **for a lie**, and worshiped and served created things rather than the Creator — who is forever praised. Amen.*" (Romans 1:25 NIV; emphasis added)

This false type of faith is not what God desires from us, and it will NEVER satisfy us. He has come to give us life and give it to the full (John 10:10) believing in His supreme goodness. He doesn't want us enslaved to a fake version of who we believe God to be. He wants us to claim freedom for our lives, simply because of who He is.

During that season where I was twisted up in my "belief," I never walked away from my faith. I didn't realize what I was doing at the time, it certainly wasn't intentional! I believe God had so much grace for me, a young girl trying to figure out how to walk through a dark season without much experience.

Yet, I caution you to examine where you are currently and your response to God through it all.

How does this idea of a false god resonate with me? Where might there be proof of that in my life?

_____

_____

_____

In what or on whom is my faith resting?

_____

_____

_____

What if there doesn't appear to be an end in sight for the season I'm in? Do I still believe He has my best interest in mind?

_____

_____

_____

_____

Chapter Three
THIS AGAIN?

Fast forward quite a few years. We had been given our miracle baby through in vitro fertilization and pregnancy. Life felt wonderful and perfect — dark season be gone! *Bye, Felicia!*

I felt like we had dodged a bullet. We got what we wanted, and I no longer had to think about that ugly, painful, season we walked through.

That is, until we decided to have another baby.

We wanted to grow our family, and at that point, we were completely open to how God wanted to do that. We had already started fostering children, and we decided to give domestic, infant adoption another try, even though it hadn't been successful for us the first time around. With an excited hopefulness, we pursued adopting a baby.

That time we went in hoping and believing that what we had learned from our first experience would carry us through.

Oh man, it pains me to even type that. Did you catch it? Where was I placing my hope? What was my faith banked on? *What I had already learned.* What is missing from that equation?

Oh I don't know... God?!

I was yet again placing my faith in something false, something other than God. The belief was in *myself* and what I had learned going through a previous hard trial.

How much we can learn from looking backward. Hindsight is 20/20 isn't it?

I went into our adoption feeling strong in my "renewed faith", based on the growth I had experienced with infertility. Don't forget, my "renewed faith" was actually just based on what I would be given.

When I had been given what I wanted the first time — which is what my faith was staked in — my faith then seemed to be proved genuine.

Remember that false theology I was talking about? I was continuing to cultivate my own personal false god — albeit unintentionally. Either way that is exactly what I was doing. I believe that is a very scary reality of today's Christianity. More of us are doing it than we even know. I urge you to stop right now and ask God if there is any truth of this in your life. Ask Him to reveal what your faith is really rooted in.

_____

_____

_____

_____

I'm praying that if what I am talking about here is feeling like a gut punch, that you are shaken in the best way. The kind of way that says, "No more! I don't want to live with a shallow faith!" I pray that you, like me, receive a reaction of desperately wanting change. A conviction of heart. A desire to learn from what we now know. "*Remember, it is sin to know what you ought to do and then not do it.*" (James 4:17 NLT)

I hope if you went into these chapters without recognizing this issue in your life, and you find yourself convicted, that you are left with a completely new understanding of faith as a result! I pray it is life changing for you like it has been for me.

Back to my story, so there I was with a "renewed faith", and once again desiring another baby. Now let me pause here, I don't want you to worry, this whole book won't be about infertility. I mean at least I assume it won't be, I guess I am still admitting God is steering this ship and I doubt I'll be talking about infertility the whole time. If that statement turns out to be false when I am done, I promise I will come back and edit it. Sound good? It's a deal.

Also, this is sort of fun, writing to you as if we are dialoguing. I've always been *really good* at carrying one-sided conversations. That is until God convicted me of not being a good listener! Talk about a horrifying conviction! I'm still a work in progress, but all the years of being a "good" talker pays off when writing a book where no one can talk back. Ha! Years of training finally put to good use.

Okay I am totally on a digression here. Where was I?

Oh yes, baby #2.

We started out so hopeful about our adoption, unfortunately, my hope was still not staked in God, but rather what I thought I understood about Him. I greatly dislike looking back and seeing that I hadn't learned from my mistakes. I'm not a super big fan of seeing how little I change when I think I have grown so much. But alas, learning is such a lifelong process, isn't it? Maybe the year I die will be the time I finally do it right. But if not — which is more likely — there is grace and Jesus.

*"For it is by God's grace that you have been saved through faith. **It is not the result of your own efforts, but God's gift**, so that no one can boast about it."* (Ephesians 2:8-9 GNT; emphasis added)

It is so important to remind ourselves that when we keep needing His Grace, there is beauty in that. Otherwise it might look like our progress has something to do with us! I *know* I have nothing to boast about, because anything I have learned is only through my own mistakes covered by the grace of Jesus. Amen!

Do you remember back in Chapter 2 when I said I wouldn't have settled for *God's grace being sufficient for me*? That's a verse from 2 Corinthians. Would you like to know what the second half of that verse goes on to say? *"He said to me, 'for My power is made perfect **in weakness**.' Therefore I will boast all the more gladly of my weaknesses, so that the power of Christ may rest upon me."* (2 Corinthians 12:9; emphasis added)

How often do you view your weakness as a thing to be proud of? Something to boast about?

If you're like me the answer is… *probably almost never.*

We live in a society where we want to have it all together, and we want to have it together now. We want to measure up. We want to be like everyone else, or better!

The Bible tells us to be the opposite. It says we should be quite accepting of our weaknesses, because it is there that God gets to show up and show off. *Does she mean "accepting" as in we should view our shortcomings as acceptable*? Girl, no! I mean accepting in the fact that we can recognize how much we can be taught through our weaknesses.

In our weakness, His power is made perfect.

I didn't know this was going to be a part of this chapter — no outline remember? But dang, I need this reminder right now in my life. Heck, I probably need it every day for the *rest of my life*!

Have you ever spent much time thinking about this? The very thing the world says we should not boast about, should be ashamed of, should cover up with a filter — God wants to use for our benefit?! To bring us closer to Him. To bring out His *perfect power.*

It's about Him.

Newsflash: *It's not about us.*

Goodness, the very minute we truly grasp that truth, and apply it to *every area of our life*, our freedom begins. There will still be troubles, Jesus ain't no liar. (Remember *In this life you will have troubles*?) But trusting Him through the hard stuff will be substantially easier for us *and those around us* when those troubles come.

What kind of emphasis do I place on my weaknesses? Shame in the mistakes I have made, or joy in what God can do through them?

_____

_____

_____

In what ways do I make my dark seasons about me? (This one is important — don't skip it!)

_____

_____

_____

Chapter Four

STILL LEARNING.

I didn't make it very far in the last chapter regarding our journey to baby #2, but you know what? God's Word came out and it was good! So it seemed worth the tangent. It's always worth sidestepping what we're talking about in order to dive into the Bible. Come to think of it, it isn't even a tangent, it's the *main point*! In fact, if you aren't actively spending time in the Bible, I'd say it is about time you start submerging yourself in it and letting God soak you in it's goodness. It is so very alive and active (Hebrews 4:12), which means no matter how long ago it was written, or who it was originally addressed to, we can apply it to our lives today, tomorrow, and in the years to come.

God's Word is **good**.

And true.

I'm going to take a moment to tell you what I mean when I say the word "good". Am I saying the Bible will always agree with what we want? No. Am I suggesting it will always feel good to read it and be convicted? Absolutely not. Am I asking you to always like what it says? With certainty, no. I feel a little like a magic eight ball just now. Back to the point — I don't need to cite a dictionary for this one, I'll just cite my good ol' dad. He suggested I define "God's Word as good" to mean: we can trust when we read it, God will show us that He has our best interest in mind, and He will reveal the role we get to play in His Kingdom.

We can trust it. The earlier we learn that, the better. We need to be able to trust the Bible as truth, *especially* when we don't love something we read in it. There are plenty of times when that will be the case, and we still need to be able and willing to apply it to our lives.

God's Word is **good**.

God's Word is **true**.

It's not a tangent, it's the whole show!

How does my life show evidence (or lack of!) that I believe God's Word is good? And true?

_____

_____

_____

_____

What might need to change for me to trust His wisdom entirely?

_____

_____

_____

_____

This is really important. If we don't trust God's Word as truth, and we don't trust that He is supremely good, we will struggle our entire lives to cling to Him when the storms come.

And they will come.

If there is something holding you back, I want to ask you to journal about it below. Then I want you to ask yourself, what could it hurt to sink your hope all in to the God who created you? On the other hand, what could it help?

_____

_____

_____

_____

_____

_____

Okay… back to baby #2.

So there I was, placing my hope in *what I had already learned*. I was trusting in my "renewed faith" that God would give me what I wanted. What I wanted, not in who He was. (I don't think the printers will allow for emojis, but I'm going to go ahead and let you visualize a face palm slap here.)

Coming out of infertility, I thought I had learned all I needed to learn in my faith while going through a hard season. Ever been there? Thinking you'd learned it all?

As we went into the process of having another baby, I totally believed it would be easier the second time around. I'm a person who likes equations, things nice and tidy, and the alternative just didn't add up for me.

Certainly God wouldn't allow us to experience the same sort of hardship, right? (Ever made a similar statement?) That just didn't line up with what I believed about God. Remember that false god I unintentionally made up? Yeah, *that one* would never let me go through the same thing twice.

I'm going to go ahead and stop right here.

Whenever we decide that we know what God is going to do or not do, or we tell Him what He can or cannot do, we are setting ourselves up for *big fat failure*. What we will end up with is not only disappointment, dashed hopes, and a confused faith, but we will have no one but ourselves to blame for it. What business do we have telling God what He can or cannot do?

The answer? None.

What are some ways I tell God what He can and cannot do in my life?

_____

_____

_____

_____

_____

Am I currently telling God what to do (or not do) in my life?

_____

Who have I made boss of my life?

_____

_____

_____

_____

_____

Nothing has shown me more clearly how I try to make myself God's boss than finding myself in the same hard circumstances when I foolishly didn't see them coming. So often I think once we've gone through a difficult experience, we assume we won't face the same circumstances again. I have come to believe this is us saying to God, "If You really have my best interest in mind, You wouldn't allow me to experience xyz again."

Whether we realize we are communicating it or not, we are often telling God how to do His job, and what we expect of Him. Oftentimes we even go so far as to draw a line in the sand that we expect He will not cross. Getting a visual here? Do you ever do that? That is us being God's boss.

It did not take long into our adoption process to realize just how much it was out of our control. We were actually chosen by an expectant mom fairly early on. I thought, "This is it! Finally, our well-deserved, easy ending!" Unfortunately the week before the baby was born, our agency could no longer contact the mom. When they finally found her, she had decided to go with an agency and family that would give her more financial security. Our hearts were broken. We had named the baby, prayed over her for months, and excitedly prepared our first born for becoming an older sibling.

Then the dream died.

I've been looking back through my blog, and I am going to use it to show you snippets of how I was feeling in the moments throughout the years. Here is one from that time.

> So often I think once we've gone through a difficult experience, we assume we won't face the same circumstances again.

———— • • ————

FROM MY BLOG...

We wanted this baby. She had been given a name and given clothes, and had people who loved her and were ready for her.

So I'm sad. We're sad. And hurt and frustrated.

I'm guessing God has decided that growing our family just isn't going to come easy. I don't know why, but I know it hurts.

I don't doubt His plan for us. It will be amazing and better than we hoped.

But this really sucks.

———— • • ————

At that time I was invested in God's plan for us, and trusting it, *but I was still equating it with having another baby.*

I am thankful for this revelation in my life *now*, even though I wish it would have come *then*. Though I'm certain had I learned it then, I wouldn't have been open to receive it. We should be leary of things we simply refuse to receive. Moving forward my prayer is that I will be intentional about trusting *God* and *God alone* in the present and future, no matter what circumstances come my way.

I didn't learn it then, but this is how I often learn — in retrospect. Even if it is a decade later!

If you're noticing a theme here, it's because there is one! I am continually learning in my faith *now* from things I did *then*. I challenge and encourage you not to always leave the past in the past. Let God bring you back to re-examine the areas where He can still reveal things in your life, that you can learn for the present and future.

Is anything coming to mind that I might need to re examine?

_____

_____

_____

_____

—✒—

Did you know that *anything* can become an idol in our lives? Or a false god?

Tim Keller, in a Twitter post, said, "Anything can serve as a counterfeit god, especially the very best things."

The very best things.

These are the good things in our lives that can be turned into false gods in our hearts, and we don't even see them coming. *How can something good become a god in our life?*

We cannot fool ourselves into believing that just because something is good, it cannot become a problem. Our children can serve as a counterfeit god, as can our husbands, our jobs, financial security, vacations, coffee, our hair — you name it — it can fill in that false god blank.

*Nothing should be our god in place of **the one true God.***

"For all that is in the world—the desires of the flesh and the desires of the eyes and pride of life—is not from the Father but is from the world." (1 John 2:16)

"Instead, clothe yourselves with the Lord Jesus Christ, and make no provision for the desires of the flesh." (Romans 13:14 BSB)

I told myself that desiring a baby was a good thing, *an honorable thing*. In Genesis 9:7 it says that God told the people to be fruitful and multiply. James 1:27 says that true religion is caring for widows and orphans.

How could we be off base? The Bible backed us up for Heaven's sake!

The problem isn't in *what we were seeking*, the problem was with *the priority we gave it in our life*. Adopting a baby and having a sibling for our son *became my god*.

I didn't realize it at the time, and had anyone *dared* to challenge me on it, I would have used the Bible as my defense. Egads! Be careful if you find yourself defensively using the Bible!!! My smart mom says, "Too often we use the Bible to defend our way of thinking rather than going to the Bible to develop our way of thinking." Wow, that's powerful isn't it?

Looking back, it is clear to me now that having another baby had once again become my priority. I didn't pray for God's supreme will in my life, I didn't pray for us to trust Him no matter what. No, I prayed that our suffering would end, that we would get our long awaited child, and that we would be a complete and happy family.

My intentions were not the problem, my priorities were.

What have I prioritized in my life that could potentially serve as a false god?

_____

_____

_____

_____

_____

How willing am I to let others challenge or question my priorities?

_____

_____

_____

_____

_____

If I am not willing to be challenged by others, why not?

_____

_____

_____

_____

_____

In what ways do I use the Bible as my defense when I don't like a possible issue I'm facing in life?

_____

_____

_____

_____

_____

Chapter Five
WAITING ON A PRAYER.

During our time of waiting for our second baby, we experienced a lot more loss and hardship. We had quite a few failed matches — an expectant mom would choose us, and then decide not to place her baby with us. It took us almost two years to finally get to the end of the adoption road.

The time we waited was hard, but the matches in the meantime were exhausting and heart-wrenching. We would get our hopes up each time we were chosen. We would be told a due date, a gender, the race of a baby, even the circumstances of the expectant mom. We would begin to envision certain life events happening with a precious new babe in arms. Then each time a match would break, those events would come around, and there we would be left standing — with empty arms. Often being asked by well-meaning loved ones how our adoption process was going, bringing a fresh wave of ache to my soul. Each time, it would build up a new set of bitterness in my heart.

As we waited, our time in Chicago was coming to an end. My husband was completing his residency program and we would be moving to Wisconsin. When we began our adoption process, we never dreamed it would encroach upon that timeline. Yet the closer our move came on the calendar, the harder the wait for our baby became. Moving to another state mid-adoption would prove a mess. It would be mounds of paperwork, more money, and cause a temporary delay in the already drawn out process.

It was enough to make me feel panicky and nervous over the problems we would face if our baby wasn't born soon.

A month before we were set to move, I emailed our social worker for an update. There were several birth moms being shown our profile and I was eagerly praying one of them would select us. Our social worker emailed us back telling me that she was *so sorry* but we weren't chosen for any expectant mom. In fact, there weren't any more moms in the program at the time to show our profile to. We knew that eventually more would come, but, of course, no one could predict how long that would be.

I was *devastated*. That was perhaps one of the lowest blows through the entire process. Our situation felt quite hopeless. I spent that morning sobbing and asking God why His plan for our family always had to be so long and difficult. I was mad, sad, frustrated, and looking toward our upcoming move knowing *with certainty* that we would not have a baby before we went. I found myself imagining scenarios of meeting new people with our little family of 3. I could just envision people asking if we planned to have more kids given our first was already two and a half.

I hated the thought of trying to explain all we had already been through trying to expand our family without losing it in front of complete strangers.

In short, I was a mess over it all.

The day I heard the disappointing news from our adoption worker I went to the grocery store with our son. On the way home I was listening to the radio station K-love. A woman was talking about how her husband had filed for divorce and she was left shocked and broken. She talked about her continued faith in God through that time and how that was the only thing that was getting her through. I was in awe, inspired, and encouraged. I stopped right where I was and broke down to God. I decided that there was no use being mad at Him. I admitted that the only way I could imagine walking our painful road was to begin to trust His ultimate plan for our life. I believed in the end it would be beautiful, so I just had to trust it on my side of things. No matter how hard it was to see.

That was an amazing experience, I felt peaceful and content in our circumstances for the first time. I was *finally* willing to let God determine the course of our path, and I was willing to submit to His will, no matter how painful it was.

Have you ever had an experience like I did with that woman on the radio? A time when you find yourself feeling so low, so dark, so weary, and then just like that something happens to shine in the light? You feel in your spirit that you've been gently lifted up, and you are reminded in that moment — *God is still here*! This, my friends, is God's beautiful providence. These moments should not be taken lightly, or tossed aside as mere coincidence. This is God working in our midst, and it is a beautiful Gift from our loving Father.

That cry out to God happened around 4pm. After that, I went home, unloaded groceries, cleaned out my fridge, and washed the dishes. The second I turned the water off I heard my phone beep. I looked and saw I had several missed calls and texts. Our social worker from the volunteer foster agency we worked with had texted me, "Call me now!!!"

My heart skipped a beat. In that moment I realized her urgency likely wasn't over a placement of a foster child. The organization knew that we were moving in five weeks and I had told them we could only take respite placements. I reasoned she likely wouldn't have been so adamant in her text if she was simply calling for a respite placement.

I dried my hands and nervously called her back.

We had been doing foster care since our son was four months old, and we were completely used to getting calls about babies, but none had ever started this way, "You better sit down." The social worker then told me she personally knew a pregnant mom who was about to give birth. The expectant mom planned to place the baby for adoption but she hadn't yet made a specific plan for that to unfold, nor was she working with an agency.

Our case worker told Jackie, the expectant mom, about us and they agreed we sounded like a great fit. She gave me Jackie's number and told me she was expecting my call.

Shaking, I dialed the number and spoke briefly — literally only minutes — to this woman named Jackie. She told me we could name the baby and when and where I should pick her up.

It was completely surreal. The strangest feelings overcame me. Did I dare get excited? Who did I even tell? There was no agency even involved. It felt a little like insanity!

Within 24 hours I was sitting in a hospital room at Jackie's bedside, and we were literally waiting on the birth of a child.

———— • • ————

FROM MY BLOG...

At 4pm they admitted her and we spent a TON of time walking and talking and watching Law and Order SVU. And we laughed a ton. I told my sister that it felt like this was exactly how it was all supposed to be. No nerves, just having fun and being ourselves. I felt like I knew her my whole life and it was so natural to be together.

———— • • ————

That was the first time in my entire life that I could remember up until then, where everything was completely up in the air and I didn't feel frantic about it. There I was spending amazing, intimate, and quality time with this woman. I had no idea if she would end up placing her baby for adoption. I had no idea if my heart would be broken yet again. I had no idea what it would look like if her family became involved, because at that point they were in the dark, and families often change everything after the baby is born. I had absolutely no control over the situation, and there were more variables than I could even conjure up in my imagination. And yet, I felt complete peace.

I was beginning to believe, for the first time, that God was in charge and whatever happened would be the right thing.

Even if it wasn't what I wanted.

This. Was. Huge.

I remember so clearly sitting in a chair next to Jackie's bed praying. The sun was out; the room had that clean — yet weird — hospital smell. I could hear machines beeping and nurses moving carts in the hallway. The lights in the room were harsh and uninviting; the chair I sat in was vinyl and squeaky. There was absolutely nothing peaceful about our surroundings, not to mention we were virtual strangers. Yet, as I prayed for our situation, I recall it being one of the most carefree prayers I've ever offered up. Not because the situation wasn't emotionally intense, but because I was at complete peace. I was *finally willing to surrender*. I finally wanted what He wanted.

I found myself no longer begging for my own plans to succeed. I began to desire what was best for this baby, and Jackie — for God's overall plan in it all.

For the first time in our two year adoption process, I no longer presumed to believe that if we adopted a child, that I was the very best option for that child. I was able to look at this woman, who I had grown to love dearly in a very short period of time, and recognize that there was so much more to this situation than simply what I wanted. This was her life, her child, and her choice. I decided I was along to support her no matter what decision she made. I wrapped the growth of my family, along with Jackie and this baby up in prayer. *And I surrendered us all.*

"Not my will Lord, but Yours be done." (Luke 22:42)

All I had truly known in my life, up until that moment sitting in the hospital, was worry, fear, and anxiety. As I faced a situation, I would pick apart each and every detail of my circumstances. I would imagine all the possible outcomes. Not only would I imagine them, I would stress over them, lament over them, and grow bitter by the mere *possibility* of them.

That is how I lived my life: season after season, hardship after hardship, good time after good time. No matter what it was, that was my way — fear and anxiety.

Looking back, I feel exhausted by it. What a ridiculous way to face my life. But I have a feeling I am far from the only one who has spent my life doing things in such a way.

How do I face the paths that are laid out before me?

_____

_____

_____

_____

_____

If I find myself defaulting to fear and anxiety, what do I gain by living that way?

_____

_____

_____

_____

_____

What could I gain by refusing to continue living that way?

_____

_____

_____

_____

How does wanting things to happen "my way" affect those around me?

_____

_____

_____

_____

━ʼⁱ\━

Friends. What can we change by worrying and fretting?

What is gained by it?

The Bible says — wait for it — *literally nothing.*

How often do we give ourselves over to worry and anxiety as a *first resort?* How often do we find ourselves facing situations with worry and anxiety, every moment of every circumstances? Do we rely on such emotions as our coping mechanisms? Do we turn to worry, anxiety, fear, concern — talking over every single possible detail of every single possible path with those around us, hoping it will somehow bring us some comfort?

All the time spent worrying, and the Bible says we are gaining *nothing* by it.

Read the passage below from Matthew and really engage with it.

Read it line by line.

> *Therefore I tell you, do not be anxious about your life, what you will eat or what you will drink, nor about your body, what you will put on.*
>
> *Is not life more than food, and the body more than clothing? Look at the birds of the air: they neither sow nor reap nor gather into barns, and yet your heavenly Father feeds them.*

Are you not of more value than they? And which of you by being anxious can add a single hour to his span of life?

...

Therefore do not be anxious, saying, "What shall we eat?" or "What shall we drink?" or "What shall we wear?"

For the Gentiles seek after all these things, and your heavenly Father knows that you need them all.

But seek first the kingdom of God and his righteousness, and all these things will be added to you. (Matthew 6:25-28 & 31-33)

Seek *first* the kingdom of God and *His righteousness*, and we will get what we need. Not always what we want, not always in the timing we hope, but God will not forget the things this life requires. On top of that, we cannot add one single hour to our span of life by worrying. Worrying will change nothing — God can change *anything*.

The revelation I experienced that week while in the hospital, began a life-changing outlook for me. I would not know until years later exactly how much it would change my entire life moving forward. That stressed-out anxiety as a *first response* is no longer where I choose to live — it's a choice. It is a choice that I flat out *refuse* to stay positioned there. Of course I still feel that fear creep in. Just this morning I felt it threatening to overtake me. But we have the ability and *the right* to tell stress where to go, to put it in its proper place — the garbage!

Or at the feet of Jesus. Yeah, that works too. Definitely.

Looking back, what did I possibly have to gain by sitting in that hospital room worrying over all the horrible, scary, possible outcomes? Nothing. *Absolutely nothing.*

What did I have to gain by sitting there, completely enjoying the moments I was spending with someone who could potentially become the *other mother* to my child. Completely trusting God in His goodness and infinite wisdom *no matter what happened*? Peace. Joy. Hope. *Absolutely everything.*

I decided I could choose to sit in a position of joyful expectation. Not expectation for what God would give me, but because whatever He decided for our circumstances *would be the right choice.*

Period.

What better place is there to set up camp?

I'll just lay it out there — there is none. This is where you want to be — trust me! Imagine you're signing up for summer camp. You have two choices: Camp Chaos and Camp Trusting Jesus. Both offer the same camp experiences, but one will leave you with confusion, frustration, and distress. The other will offer peace, restfulness, and joy. Both are camps, both are options, but they will have completely different take-away experiences.

Where we sign up to camp is a *choice.* We can *choose* to place our hope in Christ's all-knowing, abundantly loving, and divine path for our lives. Even when the path isn't clear and even when we don't know the outcome. It is there we find peace. It is there we will find freedom. It is there we will experience hope. It is a choice — trusting it all to Jesus. Choosing to sign up for His camp instead of allowing ourselves to set up camp with chaos and what-ifs. Once you've experienced it, you will *never* want to look back.

"*Rejoice in the Lord always; again I will say, rejoice. Let your reasonableness be known to everyone. The Lord is at hand; do not be anxious about anything, but in everything by prayer and supplication with thanksgiving let your requests be made known to God.* **And the peace of God, which surpasses all understanding, will guard your hearts and your minds in Christ Jesus.**" (Philippians 4:4-7; emphasis added)

Which camp am I most familiar with? What does it feel like to be there?

_____

_____

_____

_____

How does Camp Chaos affect different areas of my life?

_____

_____

_____

_____

If I haven't experienced that type of peace, how might it feel to be there?

_____

_____

_____

_____

Is there anything standing in the way of what I say I want for my life and what I am doing?

_____

_____

_____

_____

Chapter Six

HAPPILY EVER AFTER.

After the life-changing revelation that occurred in that hospital room, our beautiful daughter was born. Joey and I stood on either side of Jackie as she labored and birthed. We yelled "push" as we held her legs and we encouraged her to keep going. I can remember looking across at my husband, his expectant smile matching mine, both eagerly cheering her on. Her pain was almost over, we would all be staring at a precious baby in just moments.

And then she was born!

The doctor held her up, Jackie looked at us and said, "Congratulations you guys! Your son has a sister." Joey cut the cord and we all decided together on her name — Aida Marie Williams. It was surreal. She was perfection. She was ours. The unspoken words that hung in the air were thick and as real as any words I have ever audibly heard. Jackie had given birth, and given us a baby. *Aida was ours.*

And we all lived happily ever after and never struggled ever again. Life was blissful, and easy.

JUST KIDDING. Who in the world wants to read a book like that?!

Seriously, that would be the worst book ever.

That book would be as encouraging as scrolling through someone's Instagram feed and seeing nothing but perfectly posed children. Nothing but beautifully designed clothes, all adorned with perfect accessories, and sitting in a gorgeously decorated — and astonishingly immaculate — home. I see those feeds and wonder, "Where are the photos of real life? *Surely* no one really lives like this right?!"

Does anyone else do that? It *cannot* be just me. I don't want people to suffer, don't get me wrong, but I know what is real life and what isn't. I find myself rolling my eyes when I see a load of what can ONLY be fake oozing out of a feed that somehow has 25 million followers. Come to think of it, that's a ton of people clicking "follow" on that perfectly posed newsfeed. Maybe I am really the only one who isn't interested in seeing happily ever after, completely devoid of any sort of reality — am I?

Oy vey, me and my digressions!

So basically, no. I am not writing that kind of book, and that would not be the end of our struggles. Not by a long-shot. Because I do not personally prefer highlight reels that show what can only be partial truths, I'll keep going with my honesty.

Getting back to that hospital room, our beautiful baby girl was handed to us, and she was absolutely perfect. We spent the next two days feeding her, changing her diapers, taking pictures, and dressing her in perfect outfits. We drove her home and it truly felt like it could not have gone any smoother. We marveled over her, photographed her constantly, showed her off to everyone we knew, and enjoyed watching our son become a big brother. We kept pinching ourselves, praying it was all real, while being simultaneously extremely thankful for how easy it was all *finally* going for us.

It really was easy. That is, until we showed up to a meeting where the papers to terminate parental rights would be signed by her birth mom.

Have you have experienced those moments when one minute everything seems just normal and fine, then suddenly something happens and you realize your world is being flipped upside down right before your eyes? You have no idea how to stop it or how it is going to end. You find yourself overcome with dread, it begins in the pit of your stomach, then you feel it flood your entire body, and you sickeningly realize everything is all of a sudden very *not okay*.

It's an out of body experience. It's the worst experience. You feel yourself begging for the clock to rewind to just a few moments before, back to where everything was still so blissful. Yes, those moments, *I just want those moments back please.*

That's exactly what happened to us. A few simple words spoken, an innocent question asked out of the mouth of her birth mama, and a resultant exchange of glance between our social workers. You could have stopped time, allowing everyone else to freeze, and I can still to this day see all the details playing out in my mind as I sit here typing this eight years later.

My husband can sometimes be a little too blissfully unaware, which is wonderful for him. He sat there staring down in adoration at our sweet, sleeping, full-head-of-hair bundle of joy. Next to him sat our baby's clueless birth mama, both having no idea what had just unfolded in those few words and that traded glance. While the two of them sat completely at ease, our social workers were having an exchange of silent looks of terror. I could see them spinning the possible horrors of the situation that we had all just unknowingly stepped into. All the possible what-ifs circulated through their unspoken conversation. I watched it all taking place in a simple moment of eye contact.

Nothing had yet been spoken, but I felt it — the entire weight of the world crumbling down on top of me. I am a very observant person; I *knew* within my core that something was wrong. I felt it within every fiber of my being. I had no idea what it was, or why her innocent question was so scary, but I *knew*.

We were going to lose her.

Our precious baby was just three days old — birthed into our arms, given our name, brought home to our family. This baby who had completely stolen our hearts was going to be taken away from us.

If time had frozen, all it would need to do is unfreeze, and I would feel everything swiftly set back into motion. Our social workers would clear their throats, turn to Jackie then delicately and cautiously ask a few follow up questions. We were asked to leave, escorted into another room, still holding a baby we suddenly weren't sure we would get to continue parenting. The social workers needed to talk privately with Jackie.

Time passed.

So much time.

It was possibly only ten minutes in reality, but it felt like a *lifetime*. I texted some family members and simply said, "Please pray, something is wrong but I'm not even sure what."

My faith would be tested in whole new ways in the days and weeks to come. What camp would I land in? Where would my trust lie? From Whom would I gather my strength?

This could no longer be about what I wanted, there was a baby involved. *Her life* was what mattered now. And while sometimes I find myself wondering if my life truly matters to God (I know it does), I decided right then and there that *her life* would not be overlooked. He loved her more than I could ever imagine, and I had no business wondering if God cared. He made her, she was His idea, I knew it — He cared. He would bring us through our scariness.

I found myself being required to hand over my precious baby girl in an entirely new surrender — into the arms of a loving Father. I found myself needing to trust that He knew what was best for her here on earth — not me.

Surrendering your child goes against every impulse that comes naturally when you become a mom. Every instinct kicks in to fight for that child, and my sweet baby girl was no exception.

Instinct or not, I knew I had to surrender her. I had to trust the only One who could determine what was best for her life. He was the best way.

The question Jackie had asked was whether or not she needed to write down her ex-husband's name, since their divorce wasn't finalized.

Such a simple question.

Such a complicated response.

——————— • • ———————

FROM MY BLOG...

The social workers explained that even if G (the soon to be ex) wasn't the bio dad, he had a lot of rights because he was the husband at the time of conception. When they asked J how he might feel if he knew about Aida, J said "I think he'd fight for her."

They told us this was not a safe situation and gave us all our options. None of them involved J signing and Aida being ours that day.

They told us that regardless of biology, G could have Aida if he wanted, he could stop the adoption and there was nothing we could do about it.

Joey asked what they would do in our situation and they said "Run. Get as far away from this situation as you can." There was so much risk involved it seemed impossible it could end well.

——————— • • ———————

Completely and utterly devastated is the only way I know how to describe what that situation felt like in my heart.

Give up on the child who was already ours? Or hold on tight knowing it might not end anytime soon — knowing that the final outcome could be losing her anyway, only having grown to love her all the more with each day that passed.

When have I experienced a situation that seemed completely hopeless?

_____

_____

_____

_____

_____

_____

_____

_____

Am I in that season now?

_____

_____

_____

_____

_____

_____

_____

Where do I currently place my hope?

_____

_____

_____

_____

_____

_____

_____

Chapter Seven

HOPELESSNESS IS NOT A THING.

"Hopelessness is not a thing" might seem to be a ridiculous chapter title for a book, as hopelessness seems to be surrounding us constantly. It does in fact seem to be *very much a thing*.

Hear me out. I was in a pit of what seemed hopeless. I was about to lose my daughter, we had no end to the timeline for the journey we were on. We were certain of only a few things: 1. We adored her unending. 2. It would feel like a death if we lost her, and if possible, maybe worse — she would still be out there, just not in our life. 3. Everyone who was legally involved was advising us to run. Fast.

Those were the things we knew when I looked at our circumstances.

Hopeless. For sure.

Friends, when we know Christ as our Savior we do not dare give in to hopelessness. Loss, sorrow, and fear will come, but hopelessness is where the devil makes his playground.

Timothy Keller says in *A Brick in the Valley*, "You and I are unavoidably and irreducibly hope-based creatures. We are controlled not how we live now, but what we think will happen later."

I believe we are wired to look to the future with wonder and excitement, or fear and angst. Looking back throughout my life, my greatest seasons of fear and anxiety were when I could not foresee how my circumstances would end *and I did not trust my Savior enough*.

Something powerful happens when we choose not to focus on the outcome of our circumstances — *hope comes in*. Hope can make the uncertainty clear as day. I can all but promise hope won't make our *circumstances* clear as day, at least not usually immediately, but it becomes clear *where we are to rest* as we move through the uncertainty.

We are to rest in the Lord. "*Come to me, all who labor and are heavy laden, and I will give you rest.*" (Matthew 11:28)

Sitting in that hospital room I learned something life-changing in an instant. It might seem silly to think in one moment you can have your faith and outlook on life changed, but in my life that is often how God works. I live one way — we will call this living in the dark — for years, decades sometimes. Then God flips on the lights, shows me the complete error of my ways, and instills in me an intense desire to change. "*The people walking in darkness have seen a great light; on those living in the land of deep darkness a light has dawned.*" (Isaiah 9:2 NIV)

A light has dawned. This is the only way I can describe the moments of instant transformation and complete clarity among absolute uncertainty. A light comes on, and God makes it clear the path we should take — place our absolute hope in *Him alone*.

"But they who wait for the LORD shall renew their strength; they shall mount up with wings like eagles; they shall run and not be weary; they shall walk and not faint." (Isaiah 40:31)

When God chooses to reveal something, if we are listening — *this is key my friends* — we can expect great change. Our circumstances might appear no different, but the way we view them, and our attitude of expectancy on God's faithfulness alone can be completely altered.

That is what I experienced in that hospital room sitting by Jackie's bedside praying. God enlightened me, and transformed me. My heart was completely changed. *"And I will give you a new heart, and a new spirit I will put within you. And I will remove the heart of stone from your flesh and give you a heart of flesh."* (Ezekiel 36:26)

That quote from Timothy Keller? It goes on to say, *"Christian hope has to do with the ultimate future [Heaven], not the immediate."*

I would go as far to say Christian hope has **nothing** to do with the immediate future.

In light of the new hope I had been given, placed in God's will alone, I realized I needed to face our painfully uncertain circumstances completely different than how I once would have.

> When God chooses to reveal something, if we are listening — *this is key my friends* — we can expect great change. Our circumstances might appear no different, but the way we view them, and our attitude of expectancy on God's faithfulness alone can be completely altered.

————————— • • —————————

FROM MY BLOG...

[The morning after we were given the devastating news about Aida's future in our family]

I woke up completely filled with *hope*. Joey felt the same way. We had no idea what would happen with Aida, and we certainly didn't feel hopeful about the circumstances, but we had hope in our Savior. We believed that no matter what happened, God would take care of us and He would watch out for Aida. We knew that He had a plan and this was part of it, no matter how much it hurt.

We went to church and the sermon was PERFECT. It was all about being in difficult circumstances and choosing to see God's glory through it no matter what.

It was beautiful.

The next week went by in a blur of emotions. We heard more doom and gloom from the lawyer who pretty much made us feel like this could never end in our favor. We continued to have hope and trust in our God, but it was HARD not to worry constantly.

Aida felt every bit as much as ours as Brighton and I felt like I would die if I lost her. I couldn't allow myself to think about it because the few times I did, I felt like I was sinking into a deep hole and I was afraid if I didn't grab on to God again, I wouldn't recover.

There was a moment when I felt like God allowed me to see who I would become if I went into that dark place. I wouldn't be the same Rachel my family knows and loves, I wouldn't be the same mom Brighton needed and deserved. I wouldn't be able to stand up and praise my God because I would be too miserable to see any good in my circumstances. I saw an icky person who wasn't any less miserable for going into the dark hole. In fact I would be more miserable because I wouldn't have any hope.

I am grateful for that glimpse because I knew for certain I couldn't go into that place. So I ran with open arms back to God and continued to trust His plan for my life. All the while knowing it might be for me to lose my sweet Aida.

———————— • • ————————

Oh how sweet it was to arrive to that place. We had absolute *uncertainty* for our immediate future with Aida. I had no guarantees for what would happen to my heart through the dark, unknown waters of her adoption. But I had certainty *in my Lord*. I said I wanted to trust Him no matter what, and when the opportunity came to put that to the test, it proved beyond worth it. Trusting my Lord — there was peace to be found there. There was hope.

If we follow Jesus as our Lord and Savior, we have no business claiming hopelessness in our lives. "*But Jesus looked at them and said, 'With man this is impossible, but with God all things are possible.'*" (Matthew 19:26)

God is in the business of doing the impossible. For me that meant a complete change of perspective.

Have I ever experienced clear-as-day hope? If so, when?

_____

_____

_____

_____

_____

_____

_____

Do I believe it is possible to have hope in the midst of uncertainty? Why or why not?

_____

_____

_____

_____

_____

_____

_____

What might my life look like if I listened carefully and trusted God to transform me (letting a light dawn in my life)?

_____

_____

_____

_____

_____

_____

_____

Chapter Eight

ARE YOU ON PINS AND NEEDLES?

I'm sorry, I really don't mean to drag this out, but the truth is that what happened to my heart through this process was so much more important than the outcome. I hesitate even typing that, because how is that possible? I am talking about my baby daughter here. But it is possible, because that is the power of the hope *that* comes through Jesus!

I want to show you what the Bible says about this type of heart change, and I am going to type it on these pages in The Message version. This passage is too good to just pass by. I'll be honest, sometimes I choose not to read a passage because it can be wordy in certain translations and it overwhelms my brain. But I don't want you to miss it — I don't want you to be tempted to skip it. So I am going to use an easy-to-read version of the Bible. (Admit it, you sometimes bypass long or wordy passages in books. I *know* I am not the only one!)

Okay, here we go. 1 Peter 1:3-7 (MSG; emphasis added) says:

> *What a God we have! And how fortunate we are to have Him, this Father of our Master Jesus! Because Jesus was raised from the dead, we've been given a brand-new life and have everything to live for, including a future in Heaven—and the future starts now! God is keeping careful watch over us and the future. The Day is coming when you'll have it all — life healed and whole.*
>
> *I know how great this makes you feel, even though you have to put up with every kind of aggravation in the meantime.* **Pure gold put in the fire comes out of it proved pure; genuine faith put through this suffering comes out proved genuine.** *When Jesus wraps this all up, it's your faith, not your gold, that God will have on display as* **evidence of His victory.**

Ahhh!!!!!! I have goosebumps. You guys, what God does in our faith, as a result of hard times, is beyond anything you or I could ask for in this world. It compares to nothing! Romans 8:18 (NLT) says, *"Yet what we suffer now is nothing compared to the glory he will reveal to us later."*

Does this excite you?! I'm asking honestly. I want you to take a moment and ask yourself this question, coming up with an honest answer. No one is listening. Just ask yourself.

Does this excite me? Why or why not?

_____

_____

_____

_____

Here's the thing — *it's okay if it doesn't*. It hasn't always excited me. In fact, most of my life it has done nothing for me. I've thought, "Yeah okay, that's great and all, but I live in the here and now. Here and now is hard, and painful, so can we just focus on that?"

Let me ask you something, if this doesn't thrill you, do you desire a faith where it does? Do you want a faith where this passage sends shivers through your body for the pure knowledge of how amazing our God is, and what He alone can accomplish through your trials?

Do I want that kind of faith?

_____

What is going to get me there?

_____

_____

_____

Ah, that second question, that's the kicker isn't it? If you find yourself wanting to blow this off simply because the darkness you're experiencing right now feels way more heavy than the possible joy that is to come in the light, let's talk about that. What is it that is going to get us there?

Drumroll please...

God.

That's the answer.

God is going to be the One to get us there.

We can't conjure it up, we can't simply wish for it, we can't just try harder. He has to complete the transformation within us. But when He does, what a beautiful transformation it is!

Our faith will never be a perfect equation; we will always be a work in progress. But the first time you feel complete and utter peace, a kind that goes way beyond human understanding (Philippians 4:7), even when all around you feels like a disaster, you will encounter Jesus in such a way that your only response will be, *Jesus — I need more of You*!

Please don't confuse what I am saying here. I am not talking about a spiritual feeling that should be sought after. I am not suggesting making a feeling the priority. I am simply suggesting that when we experience an absolute peace that is so completely unexplainable within our circumstances, that we can know with 100% certainty that it is *from God alone*. This peace comes as a result of our surrender to the only One we should be surrendering to. My mom so beautifully puts it this way, "Surrender is the prerequisite to peace." Once we have experienced that type of peace, we will begin to understand how wholly and completely we just need more of Jesus.

Let's pray for that whether you've experienced it or you haven't. Let's ask God for that kind of faith:

> Lord, I want peace. Either for the first time, or for the hundredth time. Do a work in me that will transform me inside and out, resulting in a faith proved genuine. I want You to be my source of hope, security, and assurance. Search me and test me Lord (Psalm 139:23-24). I want a faith that can withstand it all, because You are a God that can withstand it all. Amen!

—✦—

As we waited out the unknowns with our adoption, our faith was standing on the only ground that wasn't shifting: Jesus (Matthew 7:26).

For the first time.

A few days of waiting to hear what would happen, turned into over a week. Jackie's husband needed to be found and a plan was required to determine what would happen moving forward. Unfortunately, no one seemed to know where he was. Everyone had *just seen* him recently, but he was not reachable by phone and where it appeared he was, happened to be four hours away.

So we waited.

Each day was so painful and grim, waiting for someone to locate him so our social workers could talk to him, so they could get some sort of idea of where he stood on the adoption. We staked our claim on God's goodness, but we grieved every minute of those early precious days with our daughter. No parent should have to spend one ounce of time grieving a new baby. Our only complaint should have been lack of sleep, not a lack of permanency.

———————— • • ————————

FROM MY BLOG...

[9 days after she was born]

I decided to go into my bedroom with Aida for a while by myself. I felt compelled to pray over her, even though I didn't know what I planned to pray. I went in sad and scared and came out full of hope and with a new perspective.

I realized that ultimately the thing I want the VERY MOST for my children is their salvation. And I can't possibly know what circumstances God wants to use in their lives to lead them to that. In fact I had started praying about a year ago that God would do His will in Brighton's life, that no matter what, He would do what needed to be done to get Brighton in the arms of Christ.

So I started praying that way for Aida. I confessed that I had been assuming that I was the only way she would know Christ, because we would raise her that way. But I recognized that I can't guarantee any of my children's salvation.

So I released Aida to God. I gave Him permission to do what He needed to do in her life. I knew He didn't need my permission, but I believe it pleases His heart to see a mother release the very thing that is dearest to her, her child, into His arms.

So I told God I would continue to trust Him and He should do what He needed to bring her to salvation.

I felt free. I felt hopeful and I felt confident in my Lord.

There is power in surrender. When we feel ourselves holding tightly to something, terrified of losing it, we give the enemy a *foothold* in our lives.

In Ephesians 4:27 (NIV) we read, "*Do not give the devil a foothold.*" In this passage the context is Paul telling the church of Ephesus to put off their former selves, which is being corrupted by deceitful desires (vs. 22). They are encouraged to remember that they can be made new in the attitude of their minds and to put on their new selves in Jesus (vs. 23-24). In the passage we hear if we are not careful in making choices, the path can lead us away from Jesus, and we will end up giving the enemy a *foothold* in our lives.

A foothold — a placeholder in our lives. I want to take some time to break this down, to make it completely applicable. This may have been written thousands of years ago, to a church in a place most of us have never been, but the Bible is alive and active (Hebrews 4:12), so this is completely and 100% relevant to our lives. This is important, please don't skip this part.

The Cambridge dictionary (don't roll your eyes! I love defining words, it brings them to life!) defines a foothold in two ways.

> 1. A noun that can be used regarding a safeplace: a place where you can safely put your feet, esp. when climbing.

> 2. A noun that can be used in regards to a situation: a situation in which someone has obtained the power or influence needed to get what is wanted.

It seems obvious to me how we can give the enemy a foothold according to the second definition, he uses it to obtain power or influence over our lives. But I want to focus on giving the enemy a foothold in our life as a *safeplace*.

Imagine with me if you will — we are rock climbing and desperately trying to get to the top. Suddenly we find ourselves paralyzed with fear. It is too hard, we can't seem to keep moving, there are not enough places to stand to give us just a few moments of security. The enemy shows up in our path, just where we are seeking help and says, *"Don't worry girl, no more searching, I got you. I am giving you a way, just lean yourself into me and I will make you safe."*

Did you know Satan does this all the time? More times than we are even aware of, he sends us a lie that says he will give us what we need to be safe. If we buy into his lie we stop searching for God to give us what we need. When we buy into this lie, we have *given the enemy a foothold in our lives.* Our enemy takes the opportunity to deceive us, and he gets us — hook, line and sinker. He provides an immediate way out, so we don't have to work hard, or *trust* God, all we must do is give in to his lie, step on his "safeplace" and settle in for safety.

My parents heard a pastor once say that as Christians get older, the enemy offers up a deal, "I'll leave you alone, and you leave me alone." We make the enemy uncomfortable when we are seeking after Jesus, and he doesn't like it. So I guess my question for all of us is, what kind of faith do we really have if we aren't making the enemy a little uncomfortable? We cannot settle for the temporary comforts he is offering. It will never be comparable to what we will find when we wait for our Lord!

If we are seeking after Jesus, then we can count on the enemy consistently coming up with ways to lure us into giving him footholds in our lives — his pseudo safe landings. Did you know before Jesus began His public ministry He went into the desert for forty days *to be tempted by the devil*. This wasn't an accident. The Bible says in Matthew 4:1 that the Holy Spirit led Him there.

Gulp.

I don't particularly enjoy that part. The idea that the Holy Spirit sometimes leads us to difficulty?

Yet, that is exactly what happened. Jesus went into the desert and fasted for forty days and forty nights. After that it says in Matthew He was "hungry".

Ummmm can we just hold the phone here? I *love* that God's Word is true and beautiful and all, but I have to laugh at the delicate way I consider this to be slightly understated — He was hungry — after forty days. I can think of about a million words I would use to describe myself if I went forty days without food. Not one single one would be a simple "hungry". You don't even want to see me if I skip one day without food! Come to think of it, maybe He really was simply hungry after forty days, maybe that was the God-part of Him. Being both God and human would have had it's crossovers. So that's cool, I've never considered that before!

I digress. So He was hungry. It says Satan approached Him giving all sorts of sweet looking options. Look what happens in Matthew 4:3-4:

> *And the tempter came and said to him, "If you are the Son of God, command these stones to become loaves of bread."*
>
> *But he answered, "It is written, 'Man shall not live by bread alone, but by every word that comes from the mouth of God.'"*

Oh snap! Jesus doesn't even need to have a great argument on His own accord. All he needed was *God's Word*. Did you catch that? Jesus was starving — I don't even know how He could still be alive — and He announces that God's Word was *enough* to satisfy Him.

I'll be honest, I don't have that kind of faith, this girlfriend loves her bread.

It didn't stop there. Let's read Matthew 4:5-7:

> *Then the devil took Him to the holy city and set Him on the pinnacle of the temple and said to Him, "If you are the Son of God, throw yourself down, for it is written,*
>
> *'He will command His angels concerning you,'*
>
> *and*
>
> *'On their hands they will bear you up, lest you strike your foot against a stone.'*
>
> *Jesus said to Him, "Again it is written, You shall not put the Lord your God to the test."*

Okay, so now scripture is being tossed around left and right, but this time not just by Jesus, it came *first by Satan*!

Double Gulp.

Does this scare anyone a bit? Remember how I said I sometimes used scripture to justify my actions, without asking God what He wanted for me? Did you wonder how in the world that could even be a thing?

Oh, it's a thing all right. Girl, it's as old as time. Satan has been using God's very words to confuse and tempt humans since the literal first people walked the earth. Is the garden of Eden coming to anyone's mind? Let's take a refresher:

> He [the tempter] said to the woman, "Did God actually say, 'You shall not eat of any tree in the garden'?" (um he is quoting Genesis 2:17 here!!) And the woman said to the serpent, "We may eat of the fruit of the trees in the garden, but God said, 'You shall not eat of the fruit of the tree that is in the midst of the garden, neither shall you touch it, lest you die.'" (Genesis 3:1b-3)

Using God's own Word is a part of his scheme! And what a crafty schemer he is indeed (Genesis 3:1a). He takes God's Word and twists it *just a tiny bit*, until it appears like God isn't really for us. Like God doesn't really have the best in mind for us. Like God isn't up with the times. Like God doesn't really know the whole situation. Like the only possible outcome is we must take actions *into our own hands*.

And honestly, how better to tempt us than to get us to justify our sins by using the Bible?

Is there anything new in this for me? If so, what?

_____

_____

_____

_____

How might the enemy do this in my life?

_____

_____

_____

_____

Jesus was brought to the desert *to be tempted*. Satan wanted Jesus to give in to what he was offering *in place of what God provides*. The enemy wanted Jesus to believe what he was suggesting could indeed lineup with God's word — and it did, *sort of*.

Here's the deal, Jesus was *perfect*, so while He experienced temptation just like we do — He did not succumb to it!

This is also all the more reason we need to know God's Word, so we can recognize the lies the enemy is tempting us with, the little twists he puts in scripture to confuse us. If we know the Bible we can get him back with our own set of scriptural bullets. That's totally a thing, I didn't just make that up.

Back to Jesus, one more time the enemy tempted Him — remember, Jesus is starving (hungry) — and He has to deal with these burdensome and tempting questions one more time: Matthew 4:8-11:

> *Again, the devil took Him to a very high mountain and showed Him all the kingdoms of the world and their glory. And he said to Him, "All these I will give You, if You will fall down and worship me."*
>
> *Then Jesus said to him, "Be gone, Satan! For it is written, 'You shall worship the Lord your God and Him only shall you serve.'"*
>
> *Then the devil left Him, and behold, angels came and were ministering to Him.*

Ahh. The sweet relief of fighting a spiritual battle and letting God's Word fight for you, letting God's truth be the ultimate warrior.

Have I ever fought spiritual battle with God's Word? If so, when?

_____

_____

If not, what would that even look like to use the Bible as a tool while I struggle through something?

_____

_____

How could I better prepare for such a time?

_____

_____

Then the angels came and were ministering to Him. The commentary notes in Matthew 4:11 say the angels came in physical form to give Him food and drink. To take care of Him.

We are not fighting the hard stuff on our own, we have an *army* that God will send to fight with us and for us. We have His Word to fire off spiritual bullets (only toward the enemy, these aren't meant for other humans, be very careful of that — been there, done that).

When we are holding tight to something that we do not want to let go of — that we refuse to surrender — it really boils down to us not trusting God with it. We don't trust that His plan is the best plan. And then in comes Satan with a convenient little foothold, *just step right here, I got you.* All it takes is one small act of settling in — stepping on that foothold — and we have just bought into the lie that we are safer in any option Satan presents us immediately, rather than waiting for what God has planned for us eventually.

This is right where many followers of Christ stay. Oftentimes we settle in and live here. Maybe we don't even recognize we've stopped asking God to help us on the climb. Maybe we aren't even aware that the foothold we stepped onto was provided by *the very enemy of God*. But even so, there we stay, nestled in for the long haul. All because when the fear came in, we frantically took the easy way out, and we didn't trust God in the surrender.

"No temptation has overtaken you that is not common to man. God is faithful, and he will not let you be tempted beyond your ability, but with the temptation he will also provide the way of escape, that you may be able to endure it." (1 Corinthians 10:13)

What am I holding onto? And what is causing me to hold it tight?

_____

_____

_____

What benefit could there be if I surrendered?

_____

_____

_____

Does Satan have a foothold in my life? What might that be?

_____

_____

_____

Honesty time: what in my life am I not interested in letting God change?

_____

_____

Chapter Nine

AT THIS POINT, THERE ARE NO APOLOGIES.

It has become clear that this story is taking its sweet time coming out.

No apologies. I will always pause for the application of God's Word.

The application of God's Word comes first. If that wasn't clear before, I sure hope it is now!

After two agonizingly long weeks, our adoption agency was finally able to contact Jackie's husband. It took a lot of sending messages through family members and friends, but finally they were able to have a conversation with him. Unfortunately, It wasn't what we had hoped to hear, *he wanted to keep Aida.*

That was the worst day of my entire life, no doubt. However I still had an immense peace that I couldn't explain. I knew God was bigger — bigger than our fears, bigger than our pain, bigger than our circumstances. I knew nothing was impossible when He was involved, and I knew He is sometimes a God of beautiful surprises. I also knew Aida was His first. And I had to trust Him with her.

Shortly after speaking with Jackie's husband, our social workers got another call from him, and he started asking questions about us: *who were we, would we take good care of this little baby, were we good people, would we love her?*

The social workers answered all of his questions as they came, and after a day or so he called with his final decision, he would sign papers to terminate his rights!!

We were completely overjoyed by this news, as you can imagine. Yet, it was so much more than just getting to keep our little girl — our faith had remained steadfast, *for all the right reasons this time*. We went through an extremely trying time with our faith placed in the right camp — trusting Jesus. It was no longer about what He would do for us, it was about Him. Period!

I had experienced a faith tested through fire and it proved genuine. I wanted more of that!

Don't get me wrong, only a fool asks for more trials, I wasn't asking for that, but I had a newfound desperate desire to stay rooted in a faith that provides peace that surpasses understanding (Philippians 4:7). I wanted to stake my faith where God — not my desires — was the goal. I wanted my priorities to remain rooted in God's goodness first, outcome secondary.

Do I desire God first?

_____

What would it look like to choose His goodness over my desired outcomes?

_____

_____

_____

_____

Chapter Ten

WHERE YOU GO I'LL GO.

We are going to fast forward a bunch of years. Not because the years were uneventful, quite the contrary actually, but simply so this book isn't a gazillion pages. No one would finish reading it.

Over the next few years we moved to another state and started our life outside of medical school and residency. We fostered a baby from birth until she was seven months old and had to say goodbye to her as she found her adoptive family. During that time we invited a single mom and her two children to live with us, learning to adapt as a two family household. The kids and I also supported my husband from home while he went on numerous two week medical mission trips.

Life was busy and we were following what we believed was God's plans for us. My faith grew tremendously beginning with that tipping point of Aida's adoption. I had begun to lean in for discernment and spiritual understanding. I stopped assuming I understood God's will for our lives, and I grew in a desire for *Him first*.

I made a lot of mistakes in this area, no doubt, but genuine faith was taking root.

After a few years of unique experiences and callings in our life, we felt a pull in our hearts to expand our family again. After years of infertility, fostering and adopting, we no longer presumed to know how our family would look once completed.

Which path should we take to grow our family? What was God calling us toward? This would begin a surrender in a whole new way.

We wanted more babies, but babies didn't seem to come (or stay) easily. This was a constant source of ache in my life. I never stopped wanting more, but the road to them had proved expensive, trying, long, and painful. Meanwhile around me everyone I knew grew their families with what appeared to be ease, in the timing they desired, and without the high costs of infertility treatments or adoption fees. I longed for a big family, I imagined our home filled to the brim with children, siblings constantly playing and bickering. Yet it had been difficult enough to grow our family as it was! I wondered constantly if we would ever have more kids, and I was afraid I would never be satisfied with only the two children we had been given.

I recall driving down our country road with my two children in the back seat and being *so tired* of fighting the same frustrations over how difficult this part of our life was. I had grown tired of experiencing the same aches and pains, and I wanted to honor God through it all.

I pulled over and let my babies keep listening to a children's CD. I turned it up loud in the back and I bent over the steering wheel. With my forehead resting on the top, I did what I had become accustomed to doing through the years — *I surrendered.*

————————— • • —————————

FROM MY BLOG...

[after saying goodbye to our foster baby]

I admit I have had some sadness in regards to having another baby lately. I am sure a lot has to do with loving and having a baby (& 3 kids) for 6 months, and losing her. Also most of my friends with 2 kids have moved onto being pg with #3, or already have 3.

And lastly, because babies don't come cheap or easy for us.

I have once again felt panic at trying to add another. I have felt sadness at a friend's pg announcement, and bitterness at our circumstances.

I am not proud to admit it. But it's truth.

However I have been trying to have more praise in my life, more gratitude for what God has given me (and He has given me A LOT).

Tonight I was outside at the grocery store and it was so crispy and cold outside. It smelled like fall, it felt like fall, and fall is my very favorite time of year. I felt in awe of God's goodness all around me. I felt enamored by life around me.

Then, as I was driving home, my heart felt swollen for the fullness I have in my 2 beautiful children.

My life is full.

My life is blessed.

My children are complete joys and I am amazed that God has entrusted them to me.

Right then and there I told God I would be okay if He chose not to give us more children. He knows I want more, but I trust His plan for our lives. And if for some reason that didn't include more children, I would trust Him.

I can remember just a few months ago my sister giving me that suggestion and I flat out said, "No" (out loud, or in my head? I don't remember lol). I simply could not fathom being willing to say those words to God. Or I knew if I did say them, I wouldn't possibly mean them.

But tonight, in all sincerity before my Lord, I said them. And I meant them.

God knows my desires, but I trust His will more.

———————— • • ————————

Until that moment, I had never given God permission to close the doors on our family's growth. I wanted four babies, I always had, and possibly always would. Two felt entirely incomplete in my heart, and yet I wanted to be grateful for them, not always living in the mode of longing for more.

That surrender was hard and painful. It felt very final, because it was completely opposite of what I wanted. Yet it was necessary. I have learned over and over in my life that the road to peace is paved with surrender. It is the only way I truly know how to let God reign in my life. Give up all that I want, trusting in faith that what God has for me is even better.

Half-excitedly, half-terrified I went home and told my husband what I had done. He is not an emotional creature like me, and I am certain he did not truly understand the immense significance this act had on my life. It was terrifying because I meant every word, and I knew God might choose for the doors to close. Yet it was freeing because I also truly trusted Him.

What is holding me back from being free?

_____

_____

_____

_____

Is there something I have been too afraid of giving up to God? Am I willing to name it here?

_____

_____

_____

_____

One thing I haven't mentioned is that after the birth of our first child, I became adamant — for years — that I did not want to get pregnant again. It had been an exhausting experience and due to our need for infertility treatments, it was financially, physically, and emotionally straining. I was so opposed to the idea in fact, that there were several times I found myself taking a pregnancy test and, while I waited those brief moments for the answer to pop up, I would begin dialoguing with God. I would tell Him all the reasons I absolutely could not and should not be pregnant again. I was certain I knew best in that particular department.

Talk about a 180 from six years before! First I was infertile and completely expecting — "in faith" — that God would give me a baby through pregnancy. Then, after being given our miracle gift of pregnancy, I all but slammed the door in God's "face" to the idea! This girl can't make up her mind (ever been there?).

Remember that challenge I gave a while back? We should not be telling God what He should or shouldn't do? Yeah, I was doing that 100%.

I wasn't simply hoping not to get pregnant, I was *terrified* of the very idea.

And it was an absolute *no* in my book.

Big. Fat. No. Thank. You.

Within six months of surrendering the growth of our family, wondering all along if God would completely close the doors to another baby through foster care or adoption, I had a very distinct experience one weekend while worshipping in church.

I was standing up during a song and I found myself completely engrossed in the words, I couldn't tell you now what the song was, or why it was so striking to me in the moment, I just recall I had the very unmistakable feeling I was standing in the presence of God. It felt like I was completely alone before God Himself. It was as if I had entered the scene that John describes in Revelation 4, being in the throne room of God. I could picture the four magnificent beasts and hear their roar as they sang in unison to the One seated on the throne, "Holy, Holy, Holy is the Lord Almighty". The song that has no beginning and no end; they never stop singing. I could all but see the 24 elders with their 24 thrones, laying down their crowns and crying out in worship to the One True King.

I was completely consumed by the indescribable feeling of being in the presence of God, there was nothing like it before, or after, that could compare to it. I can honestly say there is nothing in this world that I could ever come close to desiring over that sensation.

While the song at my church continued, my husband stood clueless next to me singing. As the experience came to and end, I found myself surprised to see I was standing next to him all along, let alone and entire room full of people. It was completely surreal.

While I stood "in the presence of God" I felt like He asked me, "Why would you close the doors on Me? Who are you to tell Me no?"

And I had to answer for myself.

I instantly felt completely humbled, facing what I had been doing for years, and taking a good look at reality. I said I was surrendering something huge to God, yet I was still trying to control so much. Standing in that moment, before God, I still did not have the desire to be pregnant again. Yet, I wanted to trust God more than my desires, so I told Him I would follow Him. Wherever He wanted me to go, I would go.

Even if it meant pregnancy.

What is something I feel like God is asking me to do that I haven't wanted to answer?

_____

_____

_____

_____

If I was standing before God's throne all alone, what might He say to me?

_____

_____

_____

_____

Over the next few months I found myself no longer being terrified of becoming pregnant. I actually experienced the feeling of being interested in trying it again. We started praying about what that would mean and we trusted God would close or open doors. We looked into doing another round of IVF. After some research and much prayer, we decided to try for another baby. We felt like the doors were open, but we knew God alone would decide the outcome.

Months later, having endured a physically and financially taxing cycle, we became pregnant again! In short, we were elated. Even though we had given God permission to be done growing our family, it truly seemed that was not in His plan after all! The baby I so greatly desired, but was willing to live without, was coming!

I went through the first trimester completely ill, exhausted, and in general struggling with the will to live. That might sound dramatic, but alas, it is 100% how I feel when I am pregnant. I experience a slight depression through much of my pregnancy, and it is much more intense in the first 3-4 months. The things we do for love, am I right?

My difficult first trimester finally came to an end and my intense fog and sickness lifted. Thankfully the rest of my pregnancy was pretty smooth sailing, minus the general exhaustion that comes with it. I felt very blessed and thankful throughout it to be able to grow and carry another baby in my body. I was just as grateful for the change God produced in my heart. I was so ready to stop telling God what to do!

> **I was so ready to stop telling God what to do!**

Where might I need a change in heart?

_____

_____

_____

_____

_____

_____

_____

_____

_____

_____

_____

_____

Where do I need to mind my own business and let God be God?

_____

_____

_____

_____

_____

_____

_____

_____

_____

_____

_____

_____

_____

Chapter Eleven

ATTITUDE IS EVERYTHING.

So now that I have fast forwarded quite a few years, I need to rewind a smidge. Is that a word you use regularly? It's one of my favorites, I know you didn't ask, but you should really consider adding it to your vocab repertoire if you aren't currently using it!

Anyway, back before we felt lead to get pregnant again, my husband came to me out of nowhere and told me he felt strongly that God wanted him to get involved in youth ministry at our church. It had been years since he had been able to commit to any ministry due to the intensely long, inconsistent, and inflexible hours of his medical residency program.

However, at the time he had this sudden "calling" (the quotations indicate a lack of support on my end, not that he wasn't actually called!), we had our foster baby and our children were ages: 3½, 1 and 6 months. Last time I checked, that's called insanity. If you're in that season right now, you're a legit hero. I didn't realize how insanely awesome I was until I lived through those years and started recognizing how much easier my life was outside of that season.

Now I watch mamas around me in those early years and I silently salute them. *Carry on brave warrior.*

Joey is an ER physician, which means he was already working nights, evenings, weekends, and holidays. *Good times*, she says sarcastically. Due to his schedule, I ended up doing many more dinners and bedtimes on my own than any married mother should ever have to endure. Given the ages of our kids, evenings were no small feat.

When Joey mentioned the idea of being gone *even more* weeknights, I flat out said *no*. I probably said something along the lines of "You must have heard from God wrong, this is absolutely not the time to start giving up any of your (ahem — my) free evenings. But sweet idea Babe!" *Better luck next time sucker!*

If you don't know my husband, he is a kind and gentle man. He almost never yells, and at that point in our marriage, he wasn't overly firm regarding something he wanted to do.

Until that conversation.

I don't know exactly how it all went down, but I know that I very clearly said *no*, and he very lovingly said *yes*. The next thing I knew he was leading youth group a week later!

I'll tell you what, my attitude absolutely stunk. I could not for the life of me understand how God could have put something so strongly on Joey's heart that would require such sacrifice from me! Did God have no idea how difficult it was to be a stay at home mom all day to such young kids, and then do so many evenings alone!?!

Honestly, whether He understood or not, I wasn't really interested in knowing. I just wanted to sulk.

And sulk I did.

To make matters worse, our youth pastor assigned Joey to a group of kids in a high school that was *twenty-five miles away*!!! People, we had a high school *6 miles down the road*, but for some reason he ended up getting one on the other end of the earth.

We had both been heavily involved in youth group before — we knew the gig — it wasn't just a Wednesday night commitment. We knew he would be hanging out with kids outside of youth group when kids are free which happens to be — you guessed it — evenings and weekends!

On top of that, not one kid in his group had a car and many did not even have a driver's license. When it boiled down to it, we were talking about him committing four evenings a month for youth group, plus extra time to hang out with kids, extra time to drive them places, and extra time to get to their activities at their *very far away school*.

Livid does not come even close to describing how I felt. I believe I might have even said the exact words, "You *need* to call John right now and tell him he absolutely *has* to change you to another high school!"

What Joey replied with I do not recall, but I can tell you that he absolutely *did* not do what I demanded.

He felt at peace.

UHHGGGG. I feel stressed out just recalling my emotions during that time.

Surrender my kids? *Okay God.*

Surrender my need for more children? *Okay God.*

Foster babies and have to say goodbye? *Okay God.*

But this — *this is where I drew the line!*

Looking back I can see how often I was willing and able to surrender control to God in the big things, but in the day to day tasks, *those* I held on for dear life. As I reflect, I can see how often I made myself, and those around me, miserable simply because I was not willing to surrender in the small things. Boy did I hold grudges when I didn't get my way! My thoughts were all about me:

"I need more help."

"I am tired of doing bedtime alone."

"I want to get out of the house and do something in ministry."

ME, ME, ME, ME, ME.

I might as well have laid down and thrown a tantrum, because that is where my mindset was.

My faith had grown mature enough at that point in my life that thankfully I felt the conviction pretty much instantly. I knew I was in the wrong, I knew my heart was being selfish. My negativity towards something my husband felt called to was gross and uncalled for. I knew Joey loved me enough that he would have supported me through thick and thin in something I believed God had laid on my heart. And I knew God would want more from me than the way I was acting.

But here is the thing, all the knowledge in the world won't change our circumstances unless we get to work on making different choices and fixing our attitude.

Did that resonate with anyone?

All the knowledge in the world won't change our circumstances unless we get to work on making different choices and fixing our attitude.

How often do we know what we should do, but we do what we want anyway? Can you recall a time where you knew you owed someone an apology, but you were too prideful and withheld it? Do you ever just know your attitude needs to be put in major check, but you don't want to deal with it, so you don't? When the knowledge of what we ought to do is too ugly to face, sometimes we sweep it right under the rug and go on our merry way as if it never happened.

Do I do this in my life?

_____

What is an area(s) I might be doing it right now?

_____

_____

_____

How do I respond when God convicts my heart of what is right and what is wrong?

_____

_____

_____

Is there a situation right now that I need to intentionally work on letting God change me? If so, what?

_____

_____

_____

_____

All the knowledge in the world, but I still had to apply it. The application of knowledge, my friends, is called *wisdom*. Wisdom leads to the change of heart we so often desire.

If we don't apply knowledge to situations, plain and simple — *we lack wisdom*. The good news is the Bible says all we need to do is ask God for it. *If any of you lacks wisdom, let him ask God, who gives generously to all without reproach, and it will be given him.* (James 1:5)

If we know in our minds what we ought to do, and we struggle to do it, all we need to do is *ask* God. He wants to give us the wisdom to grow in any area!

So that is exactly what I did. I could not just flip a switch and grow a positive attitude about Joey's decision to lead youth group, or certainly not in a long-lasting way — I needed God. Matthew 7:8, *"For everyone who asks receives, and the one who seeks finds, and to the one who knocks it will be opened."*

When we ask according to God's will, we can trust He will hear us. 1 John 5:14 tells us, *"And this is the confidence that we have toward Him, that if we ask anything according to His will He hears us."*

Friends, it really is that simple, ask God. I often have women ask me how to press into Jesus and grow in wisdom. My answer is always some variation of the same: ask Him to help you. Matthew 7:11 (NLT), *"So if you sinful people know how to give good gifts to your children, how much more will your heavenly Father give good gifts to those who ask him."*

Our God is waiting to share with us the many good gifts He has for us: wisdom, peace, joy, etc. Because of His perfect nature, He won't force on us what we aren't asking for. He waits for us to ask. If we do not ask, we will not receive. James 4:2b says, *"You do not have because you do not ask God."* It goes on to say in verse 8 *"Draw near to God, and he will draw near to you."*

How do we get more wisdom? We ask. How do we get the strength to follow through on a conviction? We ask. How do we receive the courage to own up to something we need to correct? We ask.

We can ask to receive, because He is waiting to give.

There I was, knowing I needed a major attitude adjustment, so I asked God to fix my outlook and to help me respect the decision my husband made in faith and with peace. I asked that I could not only be okay with it, but that I could legitimately be supportive! I knew I was asking for a tall order, due to the current condition of my heart, but I also knew that God is the God of miracles. In Jeremiah 32:27 (NIV) God tells us, *"I am the Lord, the God of all mankind. Is anything too hard for me?"* So I asked — and kept asking — trusting I would see results because I believed what I was asking was honorable and according to His will.

I also confessed my struggle to a friend, and asked for accountability. She shared a similar issue she was facing and we agreed to pray for one another and keep each other in check.

This is so important!

Often we let our pride get in the way of this step, and we don't let others in on our struggles and progress. Let me tell you, when we give someone permission to speak into our lives where we struggle in sin, we rip the power right out of Satan's hands to hold a place in our thought process! We can trust that the foothold will be loosened when we are held accountable for our progress — or lack of!

Exposing the ugliness within our hearts is a pivotal part of experiencing freedom in our journey! When we ask for someone else to speak truth into our lives, we are inviting in the light and saying *no* to the dark. These are incredibly intentional and valuable steps in Christian growth. The verses below validate the importance of what I am saying. Please don't skip them, even if you've read them one hundred times before!

"Therefore, confess your sins to one another and pray for one another, that you may be healed. The prayer of a righteous person has great power as it is working." James 5:16

"Two are better than one, because they have a good reward for their toil. For if they fall, one will lift up his fellow. But woe to him who is alone when he falls and has not another to lift him up!" Ecclesiastes 4:9

"I [Jesus] have come into the world as a light, so that no one who believes in Me should stay in darkness." John 12:46 (NIV)

"You can't whitewash your sins and get by with it; you find mercy by admitting and leaving them." Proverbs 28:13 (MSG)

Oh that last one… If you skipped it (I know some of you did!) go back and read it! We cannot whitewash our sins, cover them up, and pretend they don't exist. We find mercy by admitting sins and leaving them.

That's what I did in confessing to a friend and asking her to help me get through my stinky attitude.

Admit it and leave it.

There is freedom in letting someone else into our shortcomings and asking them to hold us accountable to our actions moving forward. There is beauty in that sisterhood!

There is freedom in letting someone else into our shortcomings and asking them to hold us accountable to our actions moving forward. There is beauty in that sisterhood!

Is there something I know I need to confess to someone? If so, what?

_____

_____

_____

_____

_____

_____

_____

_____

_____

_____

_____

_____

Am I willing to let others hold me accountable? Why or why not?

_____

_____

_____

_____

_____

_____

_____

_____

_____

_____

_____

_____

Chapter Twelve

IMMEASURABLY MORE.

Over the next few months my attitude improved immensely. Jesus made
a change in my heart! My husband saw it; I felt it and everyone benefited
from it. A few months into his leading youth group I was looking
back and it was then that I realized how much I truly did support my
husband in his calling. That was a fantastic feeling. God had provided.
Don't get me wrong. I am human, so I know I had my moments where
I was frustrated to be home alone at bedtime, *again*, but thankfully for
the most part I was able to let him do what he felt God called him to
without his having to hear my constant harping and nagging. That's a
victory my friends. A wife giving up nagging!? That is what I call a true
Jesus victory!

Not long after he started hanging out with his group of kids, one of them in particular really found a special place in Joey's heart. After a weekend long event with the boys, Joey eagerly came home with something really big pressed on his heart. He sat me down and began to share with me how this one particular boy did not have a family. He had come from an unhealthy biological beginning and for the past few years he was crashing on people's couches trying to finish high school and make it on his own.

I should probably back-up a titch for a moment. At this point, Joey and I had already had a single mom and her two young kids live with us for a year. While they had moved out by this time, the idea of our family including older kids or single moms wasn't foreign to us. In fact, when we had moved to Wisconsin two years earlier, we bought a very nice sized house with plenty of room to grow into, *plus* a lot of space to renovate if needed. When we were in the process of buying it, we would walk around the house marveling at all the potential for growth. We laughed at ourselves because at the time we only had one child, and yet there we were, dreaming of filling that large, old house to the brim.

What happened the day when Joey came home from the youth conference is nothing short of a God miracle. I do not say that lightly. This kind of a story cannot come from mere human thoughts or emotions. I absolutely believe it was 100% God working within us.

Joey was eager to share with me what was going on in his heart. The very fact that I describe him as being *eager,* is a tell to what was to come. Joey doesn't "do" eager easily. He is even-keeled, *all the time.* He is a slow processor and a slow mover, so the fact that he was chomping at the bit to tell me, and was filled with nervous excitement, is completely out of character for him. I had only seen it once before, and that was the night he proposed!

Joey had previously shared with me a little about the boy's story, but this time he had something brewing in his heart. He came home that weekend completely broken for this boy, Randy. He found himself asking what life would be like for him moving forward into adulthood without parents: without a place to call home, a set of parents to lean on for support, people to bounce ideas off, or a place to celebrate Christmas. Joey wondered how a boy who was soon to graduate high school would get by without a driver's license, health insurance, or any sort of financial assistance. He was wrecked for this boy and his situation, but it was almost like he couldn't quite get himself to say what he was thinking.

He finally asked if I would pray with him about the situation and I knew with every fiber of my being my answer was yes. I blurted it out, "Yes I will!" and he followed with, "Yes you will pray for him?" but my answer was, "No, I mean yes I will pray, but *yes* let's adopt him!" He never even asked, but I knew what he was feeling.

I don't recall ever being more certain of anything in my life, but this I knew. *He was meant to be our son.* The look on Joey's face was priceless. He thought he was asking something ridiculous of me, and could barely bring himself to say what he was actually thinking. Yet, our all powerful God was working the same thing at the same moment in both of our hearts, without the words even needing to be spoken.

We both wanted to become his parents.

> Yet, our all powerful God was working the same thing at the same moment in both of our hearts, without the words even needing to be spoken.

———————— • • ————————

FROM MY BLOG...

Back in Sept/Oct when Joey asked me to pray about adopting Randy, I sobbed my heart out to God that very day and begged him to let Randy be our son. It's nuts, really, because I hadn't even met him! But I knew in my heart, he was meant for us. And I ached at the core knowing he didn't have a family, and we had a family to share.

I didn't even meet Randy until the end of November, and when I did, I wanted to grab him and squeeze him to death, lol. My heart was so full thinking of him becoming my son.

It's God, I can't explain completely loving a perfect stranger! But God connected my heart to my son's and I knew in my innermost being, I was supposed to become his mom.

———————— • • ————————

Through circumstances only God could have orchestrated, at 29 and 31 years old, we adopted a boy who was a senior in high school. I can only describe that time as strangely beautiful. Nothing felt normal, and yet it all felt right. I felt like his mom instantly, and I took that role seriously. Being a mom at 29 to a senior in high school was a completely unique experience! Calling my husband *dad* to a teenager was strange, and yet felt wonderful at the same time.

Our quiet home with two small children was suddenly brimming with teenagers every weekend. Randy had never before had a place to invite friends, and we were happy to have them spending time in our home. Every weekend our house was filled with friends from the moment the weekend started until it ended.

Everything changed overnight, and we welcomed the change. To be a part of it was exhilarating.

As the weeks turned into months, I found myself truly becoming his mom. I taught him how to iron, how to clean his room well, how to scrub stains out in the laundry, how to communicate with his girlfriend, how to understand what girls *really* mean when they say they're fine! We taught him how to be a part of daily family meals, how to have conversations without the use of technology, how to chip in to help clean up, and how to do chores regularly. Over time those were the things that made us family, not *just* the love God placed in my heart — which was incredible — but those small things were what made us mom and son.

———————— • • ————————

FROM MY BLOG...

I don't just love him like a mom, I have become his mom.

My heart is so full of love for him that it feels like it is bursting constantly. I have three beautiful children that I get to love daily and somehow I will love another one soon!

———————— • • ————————

When was a time I experienced something so radical I just knew it was from God?

_____

_____

_____

_____

_____

_____

_____

_____

_____

_____

When was a time I allowed God to change my attitude and let me be wowed by what He can do?

_____

_____

_____

_____

_____

_____

_____

_____

_____

_____

Chapter Thirteen

NO MORE TEENS (FAMOUS LAST WORDS).

I remember very clearly thinking I would never want to adopt another teenager. Come to think of it, maybe it was not so much thinking it, as much as like saying it out loud — to God. It might have sounded a whole lot like the — *don't let me get pregnant God* season.

One might assume I did not want to adopt more teens for obvious reasons, teens are hard, and who adopts them? But it wasn't that — the amount I loved Randy did not possibly seem matchable, and I never wanted to be unfair to another teen by welcoming them into a family and not being able to love them the same. So my mind was completely made up, we wouldn't be adopting anymore teens!

Plus, I was extremely content with my family of (almost) four kids.

***Thinking back, when are some times I have made up my mind about
something without involving God in the decision?***

_____

_____

_____

_____

***Currently, what are some area(s) in which I might be doing the same
thing?***

_____

_____

_____

_____

Rachel, Rachel, Rachel — haven't you learned anything?!

Obviously, I had not. I was still stuffing God into a box and telling Him
what I thought made the most sense.

I have since decided God must have a sense of humor. If you don't
know, I'm going to give you a quick spoiler alert, we have since adopted
more teens. In fact, four teens total. Yes, four. Yes, I am serious.

Go ahead and have a good gasp if this is news to you, sometimes I still
wonder at the insanity of it! But God doesn't wonder.

He knew.

Shortly after Randy came into our family it seemed we had inherited
one of his friends. He was always around, and he seemed to love us like
a second family. Knowing nothing about his family, we started asking
some questions like, "Why are you always here?", and, "Where exactly
do you live?"

Without going into the details of Michael's past, you could say he was floundering.

Michael had latched onto our family and we found ourselves loving him immensely. Not quite like our son, but like a sweet boy who hung out with us and made us laugh.

Summer came and Randy and Michael were both required to return to a military base to complete the second half of their National Guard Basic Training. They would each be gone for eight weeks at different forts in the country. The worst part was that we would have almost no communication with Randy while he was gone. We could send letters to one another, but other than the very occasional and completely random phone calls for literally a few minutes, we would likely not speak to our son for the entire eight week period he was gone.

I was seven months pregnant, completely in love with this life God had given us, and I could not fathom losing my son that I had only just been given. I had already missed so many years of his life; I could not understand why I had to miss two entire months more. To make matters worse, I would likely give birth while he was gone, and I would not have all of my children with me to celebrate the arrival of their new brother or sister. I'm not an overly sentimental person, but when it comes to something like giving birth — call me crazy — I tend to be.

My heart felt shattered. I cried all the time, and I simply could not get a handle on my emotions.

A couple things you should know about me: I'm actually not normally overly emotional, I am not moved to tears easily, and I am typically very calm in those life moments when you would expect a woman to be irrational.

So you can imagine those intense emotions were a bit of a shock for me. I found myself regularly asking, *What is wrong with me, why can't I pull it together?!*

I was afraid I would have a breakdown if I wasn't careful! So I decided to start seeing a therapist. I needed help processing what in the world was going on with me. On the one hand it seemed beyond amazing to be able to love Randy so much and so instantly. Here was this boy I had not even known the year before, and yet I would have died for him. If you have children, you might know what it feels like to love someone so immensely that you didn't even know a few moments before they came into your world. If you have older children, you can probably imagine how much stronger your love for them is when you have known them for years. When I became Randy's mom, it felt like God poured all the love of those full 18 years into my heart in an instant, BAM! I was overflowing with it. Couple that with being hormonal and pregnant and I was concerned the combo might be the end of me!

I recall it clear as day, enormously pregnant, sitting there on my therapist's couch in her tiny windowless office. The couch was blue, and I held a pillow over my giant belly. When she asked me why I had decided to start seeing someone for therapy, I burst into tears over how much I loved my boy. I grabbed the tissues and did not stop crying for the entire hour. I even made her cry!

You guys, that season felt a bit like insanity. I was trying to figure out how to love him without being a big disastrous ball of emotions at all moments of the day, while figuring out how to survive not being able to see him or talk to him every day.

The day he left, I went into our basement and laid on his bed. His smell lingered in his room and I just sobbed. It felt like he had died. I missed my son terribly and no one seemed to understand how crazy that made me feel. I'm not sure even now I can understand it, other than it was all part of how God made me undeniably, crazily, protectively, and fiercely his mama.

———————— • • ————————

FROM MY BLOG...

I hate hate hate that Randy has to leave. I hate it. I wish I could make it not happen.

But I am so so so grateful that I love him with such extreme depths, that I am miserable thinking about him being away from us.

I would take the misery and pain because I love him fully over any other alternative where it isn't hard for him to leave, because I don't really love him that much.

Even though it's painful.

I am so grateful.

Grateful to have become his mom.

Grateful to have a God who gave him to me as my son.

Grateful that he gets to be in our family. That he gets to be mine.

So it will be a long few months for my heart, but I guess looking back, I wouldn't choose it any other way.

———————— • • ————————

While Randy was away, I was able to have contact with Michael. He was at a less strict military base, and he had access to his phone several times a day for hours at a time. We talked quite a bit throughout the two months. He regularly asked for spiritual and emotional advice as he went through the ups and downs of training, plus was continually dealing with wounds from his past and present life. Joey and I both grew closer to Michael through those months. Even though he was far away, it helped me as I ached with the loss of constant communication with my own boy.

Michael had experienced a lot of deep hurt in his life, from both his past and present. I poured my heart out praying for both him and Randy that summer. I decided to channel my ridiculous emotions into something beneficial. Worrying and being sad help nothing. Don't get me wrong, I think it is okay to feel deeply, but I have learned in my life that eventually my sadness needs to become productive, or else it becomes destructive.

I want to pause here. As I've mentioned, I have had no plans for this book, it is coming out as the Lord leads each time I sit down to write, so I am trusting God, and good editors to guide the final outcome! But it has occurred to me that I need to linger on this idea for a bit: *sadness needs to become productive, or else it becomes destructive.*

Have you ever taken your sorrow, your grief, your confusion and asked God to create something productive with it? Since that season of Randy being at military training, I have done it time and time again. It creates a completely beautiful peace within my soul, even when my circumstances remain painful. It allows me to be used to do something for others. Instead of simply taking from others, it allows me to give back.

There is nothing quite like sorrow to make us feel like leeches, am I right? It always makes me feel like a complete drain on my family, friends, and on society in general. Let's be honest, Eeyore is hard to be around, and that's how I always feel in seasons of sorrow.

Now, please do not hear me say that sorrow and deep heartache is wrong or shameful. God Himself knows deep grief. When Jesus learned His dear friend Lazarus had died, it says in John 11:35 that *"Jesus Wept."* Being sad is a natural, human, and healthy response to heartache. That is important and needed to be said, but now that I covered it, I want to get back to what I was saying. We all have to deal with sorrow in the ways that we need to, but I am learning that there is a time when I need to stand up to sadness and tell it that it won't rule me forever. I then ask God to produce something in me and through me — even though I know I have nothing to give of myself.

I think when we sink into despair we often begin to believe it is okay to stay there — go ahead and make ourselves at home. But the Bible talks about how good and healthy it is to be productive. Do you know the following passage in Matthew?

"Then Jesus said, 'Come to me, all of you who are weary and carry heavy burdens, and I will give you rest. Take my yoke upon you. Let me teach you, because I am humble and gentle at heart, and you will find rest for your souls. For my yoke is easy to bear, and the burden I give you is light."' (Matthew 11:28-30 NLT)

Often I think we focus on the "rest" portion of this passage. I want you to re-read it, then pause and ask yourself — whether reading this for the first time or the fifteenth time — **which part does my mind naturally attach to?**

"Then Jesus said, 'Come to me, all of you who are weary and carry heavy burdens, and I will give you rest. Take my yoke upon you. Let me teach you, because I am humble and gentle at heart, and you will find rest for your souls. For my yoke is easy to bear, and the burden I give you is light."' (Matthew 11:28-30 NLT)

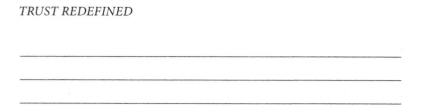

I've always been drawn to the rest portion. I read this and I picture myself sitting on my front porch in a rocker. It's a sweet summer day, the breeze is blowing, and my feet are up. Jesus and I are just chillin' there, maybe with some lemonade in hand. He is giving me the rest I so often desire.

Sigh. It feels so deserved.

Except (insert record player scratching)... let's read it again, "*Come to me, all of you who are weary and carry heavy burdens, and I will give you rest. **Take my yoke upon you. Let me teach you,** because I am humble and gentle at heart, and you will find rest for your souls. **For my yoke is easy to bear, and the burden I give you is light.**" What is this yoke He is talking about? That's a word we often hear through scripture. But are you familiar with what a yoke is?

The reason it is a Bible word is because a yoke was a common farming device used to plant, grow, and harvest crops back in the day. A yoke is a large wooden harness that is placed over the necks of two oxen to bind them together. This is done so that they may pull a plow in sync and that they may share the load equally. Using a yoke allows the oxen to pull the load together and even provides relief to either ox when needed.

So correct me if I am wrong, but I guess I don't really think Jesus is talking about a porch-sitting-lemonade-drinking-feet-up-rocking type of rest here. Much to my own dismay! I think He is saying, *there is work to be done, but I am going to help you, and in doing so **there will be rest for your souls.***

What?! Work and rest don't typically go hand in hand. At least not in my book. But here's the thing, I believe what the Bible is actually saying is: work — Jesus work — can be good and necessary and life breathing for our souls!

I am the very first person to tell someone struggling to take care of themselves, to let themselves feel, to rest when they need. But I wonder how often we let ourselves slink into that mode where we don't get back under the yoke, we don't get back to work. We don't let Jesus help us bear the load because we just don't want to face things anymore.

I was sad over the loss of Randy in our daily lives, and how hard the separation was on his already wounded heart. On top of that my heart broke over Michael's deep hurts. Being super pregnant, hormonal, and emotional, I sat myself on the couch for days and weeks crying over it. Then God took hold of me and I got *back to work*. I did the most productive thing I could do in that season of life while the time passed and I grew (quite literally): *I prayed.*

I prayed and I wept. I poured out myself for those boys, and I soon realized it was the very best thing I could do for them. I got to work, spiritually.

—∕∣∖—

I don't recall where I was when it happened, but I remember one of those days God put an image in my mind. I suppose you could call it a vision. It is never anything supernatural like handwriting on the wall or anything, but I've had a few visions in my life. While they have always confused me in the moment, they have eventually become crystal clear over time.

This image did not make any sense to me, and I initially wanted to write it off completely.

I was praying for the boys and suddenly my mind was filled with a picture: I saw myself standing between Michael and Randy, sometime in the future, and one of them was getting married. In this image, I was not just the proud mom to one son, I was proud of both of them. *They called me mom and they were mine.*

I started journaling about the confusion of this image, and I assumed that it probably meant I needed to be more intentional about praying over how we could help Michael. Becoming his mom seemed completely out of the question. Since I did not understand what I was seeing in my mind, after a few days I finally brought it to God and asked Him what He wanted me to do with it.

What is something(s) I feel God has impressed upon me, either currently or in my past?

_____

_____

_____

_____

_____

_____

_____

How do I respond when I don't understand something I feel deeply in my spirit?

_____

_____

_____

_____

_____

_____

As their training came to an end, I gave birth to my baby. We had another beautiful boy that we named Ephraim Lee (pronounced, Ef-Rum). I was sad not to have all of my children with me at the hospital, but I was so enamored with our sweet new blessing, it felt impossible to get wrapped up in that sadness for long.

Randy was home a few weeks after Ephraim was born and both he and Michael had completed their training. Michael came home first. The military flew him into an airport that was 90 miles away and he didn't have anyone to pick him up. Joey was out of town, so I packed up our three tiny children and we spent six hours roundtrip in the car picking up that boy. It was nice to see him and my heart broke over all that he had shared with me while he was gone.

There was a lot of abandonment in his past, and fear of more to come in his future.

He was a boy who needed lots of love.

Randy returned a week later and we celebrated being a family together at home at last. We found ourselves wondering what our role was to be in Michael's life, so we talked with Randy and we all prayed about our involvement. Within a few weeks, we all agreed to let Michael move in with us.

"

There was a lot of abandonment in his past, and fear of more to come in his future. He was a boy who needed lots of love.

———— • • ————

FROM MY BLOG...

I simply don't know [what his future holds].

All I know for now is he needs to be here, living in our home and letting us be his parents for the time being.

We will keep on loving him and accepting him for who he is, and pouring God's Word over his life.

Each day I love that boy more and more and I want him to be apart of our family forever more and more. But I simply cannot know what God has planned in all of that.

———— • • ————

A few months after Michael moved in with us, something devastating happened in his life. Something that severed any security he had in a prior home. We were devastated for him, and for the first time the vision God had given me seemed to be met with some clarity in our life.

Joey and I began to pray diligently, wondering if Michael was meant to be our son.

The moment I started praying for discernment in the process, I found myself beginning to love him fiercely. I found myself protectively loving him like I never had before. I found myself fighting for him, dreaming for him and, most of all, I found myself wishing he would become our son too. All the things I was previously so *sure* of regarding adopting more teens had vanished. I began to believe that God could give me enough love for two of them, and that maybe, just maybe, I was supposed to have two grown boys call me mom afterall.

We intentionally took time to talk it through with Randy and pray over it together. Just one year after I met Randy, we asked Michael if he would like to join our family too.

He said *yes*! I wrote this on my blog the night we asked him:

———————— • • ————————

FROM MY BLOG...

He deserves a family who loves him forever, who won't give up on him when things are hard, one who will love him unconditionally, like parents are supposed to! He is worth that kind of love and everyone in his life has failed him in this way, and we refuse to fail him too.

———————— • • ————————

We were all in. We went in with a fierce abandon for that boy. We weren't sure what the change was going to look like for our family, but we absolutely believed he was meant to be a part of us and that we would stick it out with him.

Chapter Fourteen
I ALMOST MISSED THE BOAT.

Just one year before, I had absolutely no idea what God was doing behind the scenes, pressing it on my husband's heart to start leading youth group.

I had no idea.

But God knew.

Randy and Michael, **two** of my children, came as a direct result of my husband's obedience to a call on his life. A call that *I wanted to squash*, that I had every intention of derailing, all because it didn't line up with what I thought our life should look like in that season. For a small season I was exhausted and because of that, I wanted to say *no*.

I don't know about you, but I know that I 100% possess the ability to throw such a fit that I can get my husband to do pretty much whatever I want.

It's not my most proud superpower, but it's a skill I possess anyway.

Do you know this superpower I am talking about? It is possible yours is not with a spouse? Maybe you possess this superpower with your mom, sister, friend, children, employees, etc. Fill in the blank with yours.

Do I have someone in my life that I know I can control if and when I truly want to? Who?

_____

_____

_____

_____

Take a moment, name them, picture them. Now if you're brave enough, I want you to picture the tactics you put into play to get your way.

Is it the silent treatment?

Is it pouting?

Is it refusal to give them what they want: love, intimacy, validation, affirmation, etc.?

Is it hurtful words?

Is it closed off body language?

Is it a nasty attitude?

What is it?

Picture it. Right this moment decide whether you want to continue being that person, doing those things, and getting your way at all costs. Even if it's *just one person* in your life, are you ready to be done with that junk?

I'll wait.

While I wait, please know I too am feeling the conviction and am texting my husband *right now* apologizing for something stinky I have been doing just this very week.

I can be *awful enough* that I am able to get my way with my husband — *but I don't want to be that person.* I don't want to use manipulation to skew circumstances and direct the choices we make for our family.

I don't want to live in a deceitful way in any of my relationships.

And yet I have been that person, I know her well. She sucks.

She sucks the energy right out of every conversation she enters into, every conflict, every overly high expectation, and every disappointment encountered. I have been *her* to more than just my husband.

If you are actively living as *her* toward anyone in your life, I beg of you, determine today to let God change you. He will, but you need to ask.

My aunt and spiritual mentor said to me recently about some stuff she was working through, "What it really boils down to is thinking higher of myself than I ought to."

BAM. She nailed it.

Romans 12:3 (NLT) says, "*Because of the privilege and authority God has given me, I give each of you this warning: Don't think you are better than you really are. Be honest in your evaluation of yourselves, measuring yourselves by the faith God has given us.*"

A massive majority of my personal issues can boil down to the fact that I think more highly of myself than I ought to. I think I deserve better, I think I am right, I think I am the only one who hears from God clearly. The list goes on. I simply think too highly of myself.

And yet, the Bible warns against this very thing! *"Don't think you are better than you really are. Be **honest** in your evaluation of yourselves, measuring yourselves by the faith God has given us."* (Romans 12:3b NLT; emphasis added)

I ask you, acknowledge to God right now if you're struggling in this area — in any relationship, or *maybe even in multiple.* Decide today if you're going to continue on in control and manipulation, or if you're going to **put on love.**

1 Corinthians 13:13 (NIV; emphasis added) *"And now these three remain: faith, hope and love. **But the greatest of these is love.**"*

1 John 4:8 says, *"Anyone who does not love does not know God, because God is love."*

Am I ready to let God do a transformation in me?

_____

How interested am I in having an honest evaluation of myself?

_____

_____

_____

_____

_____

_____

_____

I said at the start of this chapter that two of my children resulted from my husband's obedience, but then realized, *oh yeah, followed by the other two.* Egads! We ended up adopting Michael's biological brother and sister, who only came to our family through having first adopted Michael!

So actually four. **Four** of my children came through Joey's obedience.

{GULP}

Wow, that's half of my children. We have eight kids, and four is half. HALF.

I need to rewind and paint this picture, perhaps even just for myself. I was crabby, tired, and bossy. Joey was sure, peaceful, and felt called to lead youth group.

It was only because of the Holy Spirit that we embarked on the path we did. Remember how I wanted to call a veto, and Joey gently insisted in obedience? All the glory goes to Jesus on this one.

I learned in that season that I need to be open to the fact that my husband also hears from the Holy Spirit, and he has been given the responsibility of leading our family spiritually. I also want to give him the freedom of making mistakes. There might be times when he feels strongly about something and nothing miraculous comes from it, or perhaps we even later determine it was a mistake. That's a lesson he should be allowed to learn though, isn't it? I don't know about you, but I tend at times to withhold giving others the grace to learn through the same mistakes I give myself the freedom to learn through.

"My children, our love should not be just words and talk; it must be true love, which shows itself in action." (1 John 3:18 GNT)

A love that shows itself in action. I expect this from those around me, and yet, I am not always quick to offer it back in return — *especially to those closest to me.*

That experience was a huge-wake up call for me. I would have taken us down another path entirely, and with no prayer involved! *What-if* instead of the eight, amazing children I am blessed to mother, my lack of faith kept us in a place where we only ever had two? I had surrendered the growth of our family to God, but He knew my desire for more children remained. Imagine with me for a moment: *what-if* that desire for more children was never fulfilled because I was so short-sighted and so strong-willed? I could never have known that God had already planned for me the *very thing I so desperately wanted*, but it would *only* come as a result of saying *yes* to something I initially did not want.

I am extremely thankful for the attitude change, and the subsequent results, but my entire family that exists today could have gone so completely awry, all because of my own, sinful, stubbornness.

Listening for God's voice is imperative. If we feel strongly about something, and are willing to go to bat for it, it should be a huge red flag if there is a lack of prayer surrounding it!

That seems obvious doesn't it? But it's not always the case. We sometimes find ourselves fighting for what we think is best, and how often do we forget to even consult God?

"But in everything by prayer and supplication with thanksgiving let your requests be made known to God." (Philippians 4:6b)

How often do I charge ahead without consulting God?

_____

_____

_____

_____

What is something I am "fighting for" right now that I have not sufficiently prayed about?

_____

_____

_____

_____

What might change if I am willing to listen to what God has to say on the matter?

_____

_____

_____

_____

➤⁄⁊⟨⟩⟨

Sure my husband could have gotten it wrong.

But he wasn't wrong that time.

That was a time it was necessary that I follow his spiritual leading.

I won't pretend that adopting four teenagers has been the easiest journey I have ever been on, but you guys, I am so *thankful* we didn't miss this! They are ours. We are theirs. And all because Joey said he felt called to start leading youth group.

In our lives this is how God works — He doesn't lay out the plan and *then* ask if we are willing to follow. He whispers in the stillness of our hearts, and if we just happen to be listening, He often invites us into a very small act of obedience.

We do not always get to understand where small acts of obedience will take us. Often it is much later that we even begin to formulate a slight understanding of what God is doing behind the scenes. It is also entirely possible that there will be times we never know the full extent of what He was working on and working through us.

But do we want to be a part of it anyway?

What He has in store, over what we think is best, even if we don't know the result?

"No one comprehends the thoughts of God except the Spirit of God." (1 Corinthians 2:11b)

Do I really want what God wants, even if it doesn't fit my plans?

_____

_____

_____

What is a small act of obedience that He is presently asking of me? Am I willing to trust Him, even without a clear roadmap?

_____

_____

_____

Why is this so dang hard?

_____

_____

_____

Chapter Fifteen
FAST FORWARD.

We are going to fast forward through some really rocky stuff that surfaced as a result of adopting teens. For whatever reason, I have firmly felt God steer me away from certain details being included in this book, so come with me on a little bypass.

After the birth of our IVF baby, Ephraim, life was both wonderful and stressful. We had, after-all, expanded from two to five children in a very short period of time. On top of that pure madness, our additions were a newborn plus two teenagers. I'm not sure you could possibly put together a more exhausting combination! We were up early in the morning with tiny children, up late with older children coming and going, and we were woken up many times a night by any and/or all of them. To be fair it was usually mostly the nursing baby waking us up in the middle of the night. *Mostly.*

Throughout the entire house emotions were very, very high, and energy was very, very low for us as parents. There were some extremely traumatic circumstances we were dealing with among our older boys, and then the very typical, exhausting stuff with having three children under five.

I am only painting a tiny fraction of the picture that was our life in those months after the birth of our fifth child.

I am someone who truly believes that dads are meant to be at the head of the household, but even my husband would agree that it is usually moms that keep the whole ship from going under! After a few months of what felt like straight-up insanity, this mama began to lose steam.

When our baby was five months old, I recognized concerning signs of slipping into postpartum depression. Looking back I am certain it started well before I recognized it, but as soon as I saw the signs, I went to see my doctor. I was very honest about what I was feeling and she agreed it was concerning, albeit probably very normal for what my life encompassed. Reality was that our life was too beautifully and traumatically full for me to be taken down by something like depression. I simply did not feel I had the time to be inconvenienced by it, nor did I feel my family could handle my getting much worse. We decided I should try going on medication, and Joey and I were both feeling hopeful that things would start to look up.

Unfortunately, in the five weeks it took for my antidepressant to take effect, I went downhill very, very quickly. And in a very, very terrifying way.

Several extremely difficult things happened right around that time. In order for me to adequately explain how and why I tanked so quickly, I feel it makes sense to fill you in on some things that lead up to that point.

The first thing that happened was one of our older boys threatened/ attempted suicide and was hospitalized twice in a matter of four weeks. This was emotionally and physically exhausting for many reasons. Both times my husband was working and because he does not have the luxury of taking last minute time off, or leaving work in the midst of emergencies, I was managing the emotions and needs of those at home, while also trying to remain available to my son in the hospital. We had some really great help from those around us, but the burden ultimately fell on me.

Our son's first attempt was less demanding emotionally as he allowed us to be very involved in his progress and hospital stay. Unfortunately, by the second one, overtaken by hurt and anger, he became unwilling to work with us. This halted progress and elongated his hospital stay, while also heightening the emotions involved on all sides. God gave me the strength I needed to show up for him and fight in the way he needed, but as soon as I would walk out of the hospital doors, having been rejected and pushed away by my son, I would fall apart completely.

I am so thankful for my dear friend Glenda during that time. I recall several times showing up on their doorstep, without any notice, and simply crumbling in her arms. I needed support. I felt so alone with my husband out of commission and my son refusing to speak to me. The son I left at home was struggling with his own understandable emotions and naturally my small children needed my presence, both physically and emotionally.

Given it was the first time I had ever walked through anything even remotely like it, I was extremely unprepared for how to handle my own feelings through the process. I felt helpless to even do simple things like pray well for my boy. I knew I needed prayer from others; I simply remember feeling completely drained of hope. Little could I know this would be only the beginning of many traumatic, highly emotional, life threatening circumstances with our new family. At the time, it was our first time walking through the awful experience, and I felt wholly unprepared to walk through it clinging to Jesus for my strength.

During that time another good friend of mine came to me and asked for permission to speak into my life. She was someone who would pray wholeheartedly for those around her, and often God would gift her with images of the spiritual circumstances. She had long before learned that not all were interested in her images, so before she shared, she asked permission to tell me what she had seen in her prayer vision.

Did I want to hear what she heard from God? I did, I desperately did. I needed something — anything — from God, because on my own I didn't seem to know how to communicate with Him the way I previously had. I was completely drained, and I needed others to intercede for me.

What she offered was perhaps one of the most life-giving images I have ever been blessed to be a part of.

She told me she saw a series of images. The first was a field of flowers. She believed this was the life my son should have been given. A beautiful, overflowing life of goodness, yet because of people in his early years, he was robbed of that life. The second was an image of the same field, only burnt to the ground. When I heard that image, my heart sunk. It felt like a completely accurate description of my son's life, all the good, or possible good, completely burnt and scourged. I found myself wondering if he was simply too far beyond repair, if there was any hope for him to know how to love and be loved in return. Even before she shared the image, I realized that I had begun to lose hope, and I felt myself slipping into despair over what we had signed up for.

What kind of mother loses hope for her own child? What kind of mother doesn't know how to pray for them?

These are the questions I asked myself then, and honestly even once in a while I still do. Even when I still ask them, I know the answer to the question — what kind of mother? A flawed mother, a human mother, a mother who needs Jesus. Without Jesus, I don't have much hope for any of us in this world. Myself and my children are no exception. They need Jesus, I need Jesus, and I am beginning to come to terms with the fact that I will always fail them on my own. So to answer my own questions, that's the kind of mother who loses hope for her own kids — the one who simply needs Jesus. So all of us.

The third image however, was a completely different story. It still gives me chills to this day. She said she saw the field was scorched, yes, but then God began to show her new growth. Not the old life still left, but a completely new life beginning to emerge, against all odds, in that very field. One by one a new flower would be revealed, amidst the ashes of the old. It wasn't a replacement, it was a *rebirth*.

She believed God was giving her a message for me. Though perhaps my boy's life would be entirely burned to the ground, it was all for the purpose that He could begin to heal and feel loved again. God would not let my son's earlier life and wounds be for nothing. God — and God alone — could redeem the mess that had been done to my poor boy's heart. There could be hope, because through Christ, there is always hope. Always.

"But Jesus looked at them and said, 'With man this is impossible, but with God all things are possible.'" (Matthew 19:26)

My boy was lost, but he would be found.

"For the Son of Man came to seek and to save the lost." (Luke 19:10)

There was devastation, and complete destruction done to his life, but our God of hope is also a God of miracles. He had His sights set on my boy, and He alone would be his redemption.

I was not the answer, *Christ was.* I was not his hope, *Christ was.* I would not be his salvation, *Christ would be.* I did not need to worry, or fear, because that is what we have a Savior for.

"Cast all your anxiety on Him because He cares for you." (1 Peter 5:7 NIV)

I ended the call with my friend and I was a new woman.

I had found freedom that I didn't even know existed. There was *no need* for me to know the outcome of my son's circumstances or his heart. All I needed to do was trust that God knew, *and I could rest in that.* I still had emotions to deal with due to the nature of our life and the season we were in, but that profound freedom I experienced with that particular son has not wavered since. God is in charge of my boy, and I can rest in that.

Do I believe that God knowing the outcome is all that matters? Why or why not?

_____

_____

_____

_____

_____

What could change if I lived my life with the assurance of God alone knowing the outcome?

_____

_____

_____

_____

_____

—⁄❡▹—

The second major event that happened during that same season of postpartum depression was a near death experience with one of our younger children. Brighton has asthma and as a result, has often reacted very poorly to a common cold.

We have had protocols in place to help navigate his breathing at home through such circumstances, but that one particular time, nothing we did seemed to help. My husband — an ER physician — is no stranger to emergencies. Due to his knowledge and skill set, we rarely ever take our kids to the hospital. That time was different. I could see the fear growing in Joey's eyes as he monitored Brighton's oxygen levels, and administered the appropriate treatments, all to no avail. Our son was declining rapidly and Joey finally said it was time to take him in. After a few hours in the ER, it was clear that they were not able to make progress getting more oxygen into his lungs either, and he was admitted to the hospital.

We watched the doctors work through the night, but despite administering all the correct treatments, and tests run, there did not appear to be an obvious answer for what was keeping his lungs from receiving a healthy amount of oxygen. Nothing showed on a scan, but there was something obstructing the way, and he was growing more and more critical with each passing hour. My husband is an extremely calm and even-keeled man, as I have mentioned. This is what makes him an incredible doctor to be in charge of emergencies and traumas. As I watched him completely unraveling in fear, we all knew it was a strong indicator that something was really wrong with our little boy.

It was determined that Brighton needed more help than our local hospital could give him and he would be transported by ambulance to a children's hospital in Minneapolis, Minnesota. My husband rode along with him because he would be the only person in the next hour that was trained to intubate him, should that become necessary. Where things were headed, that seemed entirely possible.

As Brighton was getting ready to be transferred, we feared as bad as things were, that we might be facing our last few days with him. A little body like his could simply not continue to live without getting sufficient oxygen. It was devastating watching how hard he was working and how small of an impact it was producing. His body was completely weak, lethargic, and depleted.

My mom sent a group message to everyone she could think of, asking that at exactly 1:00 p.m. they would all collectively pray for a miracle. Brighton was to be transferred at that time and she felt strongly that is when he needed intense prayer.

According to Joey, about fifteen minutes into his ambulance ride, Brighton started coughing from the bumps in the road and all of a sudden, like a miracle, his lungs started receiving oxygen! By the time he arrived at the children's hospital, we were looking at a much healthier child! He was far from out of the woods, but he was definitely moving in the right direction. Before the ambulance ride he was too sick to speak more than a word or two, and fifteen minutes after his miracle, Joey sent me a video of him saying in a still weak, but sweet voice, "I'm feeling a little better mommy!"

You guys, I want to be completely honest with you, before that time I believed in prayer, I really did. But I did *not* believe in prayer like that. I had never seen anything like that before and I know that God completely granted us a miracle, one that I'm quite convinced might not have happened had we not all been praying so fiercely.

There was no medical answer for why he was not receiving oxygen, they had run all the tests, yet during the exact time period that groups of people were collectively praying for a miracle, we received one.

Now, I need to say, I do not believe that our healing on this earth is dependent on our faith. I believe that when the Bible tells us to ask anything in His name and it can be granted to us, that it is only done so when it is in accordance with His will (1 John 5:14). I also do not believe that we are intended to live a pain free life on this earth. Remember the "promise" Jesus gave us back in Chapter 2 — John 16:33? Trials are inevitable. So there are times when due to the fallen world we live in, we are not granted miracles.

I also do not claim to understand the ways of God. Deuteronomy 29:29a says, "*The secret things belong to the LORD our God.*" I do know that there are things we will ask for on this earth and for reasons we might not understand, they will *not* be in accordance with His will (Acts 4:28). There are trials that we will have to endure, and Romans 8:28 tells us that God will work them together for the good of those who love Him.

As for my son Brighton, I had begun to wonder if losing him might be part of God's plans for our life. I was not "okay" with that, of course, what mother could be? But I felt myself trusting His supreme power over my boy. I am completely aware that making such a statement on this side of things is "easy". Had I been asked to live through the loss of my son, I likely would have struggled a million times over with that same truth. However, loss or no loss, it is truth nonetheless. Our God is a sovereign God, and He alone writes the plans. "*For my thoughts are not your thoughts, neither are your ways my ways, declares the Lord. For as the heavens are higher than the earth, so are my ways higher than your ways and my thoughts than your thoughts.*" (Isaiah 55:8-9)

After Brighton's miraculous turn of corner, I had someone very close to me share with me that while she and her husband were praying for him, they felt consumed with a very dark cloud, something they felt covered their bodies, hearts and souls, and they both instantly believed that our son was going to die. They couldn't reason the experience any other way. They said within the fifteen minutes that they were praying, they suddenly felt the darkness lift and experienced what felt like a cloud parting ways and light coming through. They both had the same belief that God was saying He would save our son. I asked for more details and she said she did not 100% know how to interpret it other than it felt like they had spiritually experienced a change of outcome.

After hearing this, and knowing the sincerity of these two individuals, I decided to go to my friend I mentioned earlier — the one with the powerful prayer images. I asked her if she had anything she could offer on his miracle. She had been previously trained to never reveal if she saw a death or a birth through prayer in someone's life. Trusting that to be wise, she never did. However this time was different, our son had lived and I wanted to know if she had seen anything in her prayers. Without telling her what the other two had told me, she shared with me that she had indeed seen him in her images. He was lying there, dead, and within the span of fifteen minutes, she believed God showed her that He planned to save him.

Even writing this, all these years later, it feels impossible to grasp what in the world was happening in the spiritual realm during that day. I am sure I won't ever know the fullness of it this side of Heaven, but what I have concluded is that my son was going to die, and God decided to spare him. I don't know the reason, I don't know His purposes for my boy, or this story, but it has shown me the incredible power of prayer in ways I had never experienced before.

We all prayed and he lived. However, I also believe it is possible that we could have prayed and he might have still died. This is a very hard pill to swallow. Prayer works, but God is not a genie. He does not always answer the way we think. We live in a fallen world, so there will be pain and suffering. Until the coming of the new earth (Revelation 20-22), or we walk the streets of Heaven, we will not escape tragedy. That is a direct result of sin in our world.

The Lord's ways are a mystery to mankind, but I trust them to be right. *"As you do not know the way the spirit comes to the bones in the womb of a woman with child, so you do not know the work of God who makes everything."* (Ecclesiastes 11:5)

I also believe that when we don't ask, we don't receive.

A collective group of believers is a powerful thing that is not to be dismissed. *"Again I say to you, if two of you agree on earth about anything they ask, it will be done for them by my Father in heaven. For where two or three are gathered in My Name, there am I among them."* (Matthew 18:19-20)

If there are times I don't ask others to join me in prayer, what holds me back?

_____

_____

Do I believe that when we pray together it can change things?

_____

_____

How do I handle it when the answer doesn't come as I hope?

_____

_____

—✦✦✦—

During the season leading up to my postpartum depression, as you have seen, I had already experienced some extreme circumstances in my family, and all within a two month period. Emotions were high, energy was low, but God had continued to be faithful. He gave us what we needed to get through each trial, trusting His goodness and His supremacy in our life. I did not know if our son Brighton would have another unexplained life-threatening episode, but I knew God had carried us through it and the last thing I should do moving forward was to live in fear.

Fear is no doubt the natural default response for most of us when we walk out of a scary situation. I don't know about you, but I think it is actually *easier* and more natural to live *in fear* than it is to fight against it. At the time however, I could reason that fear was not what my family needed from me. Remember what Matthew 6:27 (NLT) says? *"Can all your worries add a single moment to your life?"* Worrying wasn't going to change the future. Prayer might, but worry would not. We could not predict if in the future we would find ourselves fighting the same battles over the lives of our two sons. If we did, worry and fear would do nothing to prepare us for the repeated circumstances.

What are some evidences in my life that I might believe worrying is beneficial to my future?

_____

_____

_____

_____

_____

_____

What could change if I began to let God reshape my thinking in this area?

_____

_____

_____

_____

I could have lost my sons. Yes. Both of them. But I did not, and the only healthy response should be gratefulness and a deliberate fight against the enemy as he threatens to steal my joy with *fear*.

The definition of fear, according to the English Oxford Dictionary, is the opposite of trust:

An unpleasant emotion (ain't that the truth!?) *caused by the belief that someone or something is dangerous, likely to cause pain, or a threat.*

If we give into fear, it is like we are saying,

> "God I believe You are dangerous, likely to cause me pain, or You are a threat to my life."

When we don't know the outcome in life, or our circumstances, but we choose to trust Him anyway, we are saying,

> "God I firmly believe You are reliable, You are truth, You are able, and You are safe."

Fear not is recorded over 70 times in the Bible. Regularly God reminds His beloved children to "fear not", or to "not be afraid". In case it isn't inherently obvious, I will piece it together in the way that makes sense to me.

We are His children, He understands how all the life puzzle pieces fit together. He has the intimate knowledge of how the *entire* world began, has gone, and will end. He knows that He is 100% perfect and 100% good and 100% trustworthy and 100% able and 100% safe. *Anything* other than putting our fear aside, and grabbing onto HIS plans in trust is… I'm going to say it… *utter lunacy.*

Fear, my friends, will exhaust us, grieve us, tear us down, and beckon us away from Jesus. Fear is a distraction by the enemy, designed to ruin us and our trust in our Creator.

Did you know this? Have you experienced the feeling of complete depravity of joy, peace, and faith? That is what fear leaves us with. It has consistently been one of the most exhausting parts of my life. I don't know about you, but fear leaves me completely drained. When our world was created perfect, there would have been no need for fear. It was only after the deception of the enemy that it entered the equation.

Stopping to consider that fear is a distraction from the enemy, in what ways is this news to me?

_____

_____

_____

_____

How does this distraction take my focus away from trust in God?

_____

_____

_____

_____

―✱―

Fear is from the enemy. Freedom is from our Creator.

God knows what is to come, He knows when it will happen, and He knows how you and I will survive it. He knows because He will be there right with us the entire way.

"Fear not, for I am with you; be not dismayed, for I am your God; I will strengthen you, I will help you, I will uphold you with my righteous right hand." (Isaiah 41:10)

He is waiting for us to ask for His help, He is eager to free us from fears, He alone will be the One to deliver us from them. You and I are NOT meant to make our home among fear.

"I sought the Lord, and He answered me and delivered me from all my fears." (Psalm 34:4)

Deliverance from fear is an option! Freedom is from our creator.

What are some warning signs that fear can wreak havoc on a healthy life?

_____

_____

_____

_____

Do I want to do the work to live proactively — in faith and prayer — fighting fear as an enemy in my life? Why or why not?

_____

_____

_____

_____

I had a choice: should I place my energy in the fear of not knowing what the future would hold for my boys? Or would I surrender that fear — that unknowing — and let God be God and determine to keep me as me?

I chose trust.

I chose it then and I choose it now. I decided to believe that God had a better way, *even if* it included pain and uncertainty along the way. I refused to live in fear of those *what-ifs*. I reasoned that I would never regret the days I chose to trust and I was certain I would regret wasting years of my life living in fear.

Fear entered the human race as a result of the fall, and I believe we are all tempted to live in it. It is a distraction meant to keep our eyes from remaining focused on Jesus. I have this mental picture of the devil himself speaking to his minions and I can just imagine him saying something like this, "As long as we keep them afraid, they will never be free. If they never feel free, they will not grow the kingdom of God."

Whether we know it or not, we choose one way or another. Not living in fear is a deliberate and intentional decision. I'll use the analogy of a river, if we are not actively swimming against the current, we are being taken downstream with it. Fear is much like this, if we are not actively working against its place in our lives, we will be taken "downstream" with it.

I was reading to my five-year-old the other night about the time Jesus calmed the storm. Often when reading that story we focus on the fact that Jesus was sleeping during the storm, or the fact that He merely spoke human words and the wind and waves obeyed Him. But on this particular night, snuggled up with my little buddy on his bed in an attic corner, I was completely hung up on the last part. He took care of the mess, turned to His disciples and asked them, "*Why are you so afraid?*

Have you still no faith [trust]?" (Mark 4:40)

Jesus was human, so He would have understood the dire circumstances they were facing, a storm that size could have capsized their boat and killed them all. But He was also God, and that meant they had God in the boat with them. That left only one logical question in His mind, "Why in the world would they be so afraid?"

If we truly believe He is the God of the universe, the Creator of mankind, the Savior of the world, why would we ever need to be so afraid? Unless we still have so little faith.

Fear = lack of faith. Jesus said so.

"Why are you so afraid? Have you still no faith?" (Mark 4:40)

What fears am I living with that need to be turned around and into trust?

_____

_____

_____

_____

_____

Where will I place my trust?

_____

_____

_____

_____

_____

_____

Chapter Sixteen

TRIAL AFTER TRIAL.

While in the midst of all the uncertainty with two of our boys, we battled a third trial that was especially difficult on my heart. I was exclusively breastfeeding our baby Ephraim. Nursing had been an extremely successful experience with our first biological child, Brighton. Brighton had been a nice round baby who seemed to get plenty fed. I nursed him with little to no issues until he was 22 months old. I honestly could not have asked for a better breastfeeding relationship my first time around.

Naturally, I assumed it would be the same with subsequent babies. However, around 4-5 months old, it became concerning to our pediatrician that Ephraim was no longer gaining weight. In fact he began to rapidly fall off the growth chart. He was born somewhere around the 40th percentile, and ended up getting as low as the 2nd percentile. We embarked on all sorts of paths to try and help him gain weight while on my milk, but nothing seemed to help. Weekly weight checks and constant monitoring lead to more and more discouragement, especially on my part since I was the one solely responsible for feeding him.

If there is anything mothers tend to take to heart, it is the responsibility of creating, growing, birthing, and feeding babies. I have friends who have never been able to successfully conceive or breastfeed, and while some of them were able to become mothers in other ways, or chose other methods of feeding their infants, some have admitted struggling against the lie that they are not "real women". Of course logically, our worth as women has nothing to do with what our bodies can produce. Our success in how we grow our families or feed our babies has absolutely no merit whatsoever on whether we are "real women" or not. And yet, it is an easy and clever way for the enemy to sneak in and make women question who they are and where their worth lies. I was no exception.

I had already walked through infertility, and lacked the ability to conceive in the natural, "God-given" way. Suddenly finding myself additionally unable to give my new baby what he needed, in the way God had literally designed the female body to do, was like a gaping wound to my soul. As I watched him fall off the growth charts, not successfully manage to gain weight, and become dangerously close to being diagnosed with "failure to thrive", I felt like a complete failure. I questioned my ability as a mother in more ways than one, and I found myself emotionally falling apart, no matter how strong I tried to remain.

I had had enough. It felt like one attack after another and everything around me seemed to be crumbling.

I wanted to help my family through the trials, and I was trying so hard to rely on Jesus! But something had to give. That was when I went to meet with my doctor, and we made the decision for me to go on medication. After trying all else with Ephraim, we finally switched him over 100% to formula — against my aching heart — and we prayed we might finally have set course on the right track for all of us.

Over the next five weeks while I waited to feel better on my antidepressant, we experienced one final blow in our family, and it became clear I might not survive that one.

One of our older sons started pulling himself away from us. I sensed it building up for months; the family trials were taking a toll on him. It is natural for kids who are finally adopted into a family to think that having a healthy family will be nothing but blissfully wonderful. Our children are no exception. After almost losing a sibling and watching another one battle severe depression and repeated suicidal attempts, our son started to question if it was really worth the risk. Is it worth it to love people who might fail you, leave you, or die on you?

The distance started small, but I felt it in my heart enormously. I clung to him harder than ever, clawing for control in his life and in our family. As you can probably imagine, my clinging for control only pushed him further away. The more I pushed for a place in his life, the more he ran away from us. The more he ran, the harder I pushed. It created a destructive cycle downward, and with my own emotional instability, I seemed to have lost all sense of logic regarding how to love our boy as he struggled through his questions and concerns about our family. Before we knew it, he was no longer coming home. We didn't know where he was, what he was doing, or who he was with.

Finally he shut us out completely. He needed to run and he needed to be apart from us. He cut off all forms of communication, even with those around us who might have been able to help us connect with him. We were completely in the dark when it came to his life.

Already teetering on the edge of complete destruction, that rejection shoved me full blown into a darkness I had never experienced before.

I had previously been very close to our son. I not only believed he needed us, I began to realize how much I *needed him*. I had become extremely attached to him, and my worth as a mother had become entwined with how well he was doing in life. Through all our struggles prior to that season it appeared that we were on the right track with him. *He was our win.* From all outward appearances, it looked like he was the only one that wasn't falling apart. Somehow that became an idol in my life. *As long as this son is doing okay, then we will be okay. As long as he is good, we can know that we have done something right.*

I didn't speak those exact words out loud, because I honestly didn't even know I felt that way at the time. Only in examining my heart in retrospect, can I see that I completely believed them.

I made my son — and our relationship — the glue that was holding our fragile family together.

It sickens me to even say it — to even type the words. I made my son the glue that held our family together. Not only do I know that *Jesus* should be the *only* glue that holds us together, what an awful and ridiculous expectation to place on another person, *let alone a child.*

No person should have to bear such a load of responsibility. No person can be responsible for our saving. Only Jesus should be given that role in our life.

It is possible you're on the other side of these pages thinking, *how could she have believed that he was their glue? How could she have pushed away her own son?* But here's the thing, I know I am not the only one who has ever done this. I would be shocked if you didn't find you had your own form of unhealthy glue in your life. Maybe your glue isn't a child, maybe it's your mom, your sister, your spouse, or your friend. Maybe it is security in your job, your community, your church, or a financial situation. Whatever it is, I believe in our flesh we all have a tipping point — we all have that one thing that we are tempted to make an idol in our lives in such a way. *As long as this person, or this thing, is intact, I will be okay…*

No person other than Jesus can be responsible for our saving.

Is there someone or something in my life that I have given this role to? If you're willing, write it down and confess it to God.

_____

_____

_____

_____

What are some unintentional idols I have in my life right now?

_____

_____

_____

_____

—/|\—

I will tell you what happened when my son left our family, blocked us and everyone we knew from having any communication with him — *I completely shattered.* I did not even unravel. No, unraveling is a slow process, one that can be seen and measured.

I shattered.

It was as if in one fell swoop everything I believed about myself and my place in this life was smashed at the center and collapsed to the ground in a purposeless, pitiful heap.

I felt a swarming dark presence envelope me, beckoning me to be taken down with it into a deep, dark pit. Encouraging me to make myself at home there, to set up shop there, and never leave. I was welcomed into a darkness that I previously hadn't even known existed, and in the scariest of ways possible — *I liked it there.*

For the next few weeks I laid prostrate on the hard, unwelcoming, ground as a useless heap of a shattered person.

I did not open the curtains.

I did not uncover my head.

I did not stop crying.

I did not have hope.

I did not feel I mattered.

I did not view my life worth living.

I did not trust myself to be alone.

I did not have the will to live.

I felt like King Solomon in Ecclesiastes when he wrote, "*Meaningless! Meaningless! Utterly meaningless! Everything is meaningless.*" (Ecclesiastes 1:2a NIV)

My family stepped in and saw me drowning. They begged me to get up and fight. They begged me to care. They begged me to see my other four children as worth living for.

But the problem was, it wasn't about them, it was about me. I could no longer see any good within me. I could no longer imagine that my children's lives were better with me in it.

I simply wanted to cease to exist.

Satan had taunted me with a lie — that life was no longer worth living, and with every fiber of my being I believed it.

Of all the trials I had experienced up until that point, that one was the scariest. Not because I think the loss of my life would have been worse than anyone else's. No, it was because that time felt like a literal fight for my life, and it was against *the devil himself.*

It was a fight, but I wasn't even fighting. I was literally lying down and letting Satan win.

I had given up, and for the first time in my entire life, nothing seemed to matter.

That season was *so dark* and *so scary* that sometimes I cannot even recall how it ended. It is such a dark cloud in my memories, it's painful to look back and even see clearly through the lens of darkness that encompassed my mind. It's easier to remember it as if all of a sudden things were simply better, as if one day I woke up from a really bad dream, and I began to feel like myself again.

Except that isn't how it happened.

While dissecting this season, and the condition I was in, I found myself asking, "How in the world did I get better?!" I know it had to have been Jesus, but how did He get me from point a to point b?

Then God made it clear: *It was those around me.* He used them to save me.

If it were not for them and their determination to fight for me, I would have taken my own life.

That's the honest to goodness truth.

I wanted to cease to exist and I fantasized about ending my own life.

I said it was the others who saved me, but the worst part is — I didn't even want to let them save me. How is that for crazy?

Is there a time I needed saving in my life, but didn't want to receive help? If so, when?

_____

_____

_____

_____

Let me tell you something I am *really really* good at: It's pushing others away. I come from a healthy background, a healthy family, a healthy childhood, so why it ever started, I am not really certain. But, if there were a grading scale for pushing people away, I would be close to acing the test.

Pushing others away is a really ugly trait. It feels ugly on the inside of it, and I *know* how hard it is to love someone from the other side of it. When you just want to help someone who is struggling immensely, and they refuse to give you an inch in their life, it's exhausting, frustrating, and defeating.

I can tell you candidly now that I am good at pushing people away, but for a long time I actually didn't know this about myself. I could feel the tension I caused regularly in relationships, but I couldn't really pinpoint exactly what the problem was. Maybe I didn't want to face it, maybe I didn't want to ask myself the hard questions, but whatever it was, I felt it within — we always do. Thankfully years of maturing and growing in my faith, studying the Bible, and letting God examine my heart, has brought me some answers for why I push others away. I now know, with great certainty, that pushing others away is actually rooted in a form of pride. *You don't know what I am going through. You don't know what this feels like, so you can't help me.*

Me, me, me, me, me.

The definition of pride according to the English Oxford Living Dictionary is: *the quality of having an excessively high opinion of oneself or one's importance.* This excessively high opinion of ourselves, believe it or not, can even be attached *to our trials.*

When we push others away because they can't possibly understand our circumstances, or could *never imagine* how we feel, our pride is essentially saying, "My hurts are more than your hurts. My wounds are more important than your wounds. So I cannot let you in because you don't measure up."

When we need someone more than ever, but we refuse to let them get close enough to help — that is our pride rearing it's lovely head.

If you're sitting there with this book in your hands and you *know* you push others away, have you ever stopped to consider it's rooted in sin? Or maybe you're suddenly, just in this very moment realizing that you push others away. Can you stop to digest what I am saying — ask yourself if this is you? Maybe you push others away, and you want them to come chasing after you. That's pride. Maybe you push others away and you give them the silent treatment, but you expect them to beg for a hearing with you. That's pride. Maybe you push others away and you never even look back, you don't even pray for resolution and healing. That's pride.

Pride is a deeply rooted sin that manifests itself in tricky ways, ways that are sometimes difficult to pinpoint. Don't be fooled, tricky or not, it doesn't change the fact that pride is still pride, and pride is still sin.

Do I recognize the ways that I have hidden (or not-so-hidden) pride in my life?

_____

_____

_____

_____

_____

_____

Am I willing to face my pride, confess it to God, and let Him begin the process of rooting it out of me?

_____

_____

_____

_____

_____

_____

If I don't know the areas, I ask You Lord to reveal an area to me that I have been blind to.

_____

_____

_____

_____

_____

_____

Chapter Seventeen

NOW WHAT?

I wonder how many finished that last chapter and are thinking to themselves, *Thank you Rachel for that lovely little reveal. I could have gone my entire life without the sinful pride in my heart having been pointed out.* Raise your hand if you're feeling a little bit that way. Or maybe you're saying, *um, I know all about my pride and I am just fine with it thank you very much, mind ya own business.*

I see you, both of you. You're in good company, I've totally be there. Friends, the Bible says, *"Pride goes before destruction, and a haughty spirit before a fall."* (Proverbs 16:18) Let me tell you, pride is the beginning of the end of us. It goes before our *own destruction.* Sure it hurts others, but it starts by hurting us! Pride tells us, "You are strong, that is why you feel this way. You don't let others push you around, or tell you what to do." Yet the destruction that continually follows our prideful thoughts, actions, and ways, speaks for itself. It's garbage and we should want no part of it in our lives!

"Do you see a man who is wise in his own eyes? There is more hope for a fool than for him." (Proverbs 26:12)

Pride is quite possibly one of the worst sins. Of course I don't mean worst on the rating scale — sin is sin — I mean worst in the sense that I see it as a gateway sin. If we don't recognize pride in our life and we let it go unchecked for months, years *or decades*, we can be sure that it will creep into every single nook, cranny, and corner of our lives. It will leak into our relationships, our ministries, our families, and our every thought process.

People say things like, "I have a lot of pride" — as if that is a good thing. *Pride is not a good thing.* Pride always has a destructive and negative spiraling effect in our lives.

Psalm 10:4 says that proud people are so consumed with themselves that it leaves no room for God in their thoughts, *"In the pride of his face the wicked does not seek Him; all his thoughts are, "there is no God."* William Law says in his book *The Spirit of Prayer*, "If you could see what every stirring of pride does to your soul, you would beg of everything you touch to tear the viper from you, even if it required the loss of a hand, or an eye."

That's intense people. Intense.

Beg to be rid of it — the viper of pride.

For years, and honestly even decades, I did not recognize pride in my life. I did not recognize it for what it was — the devastation of everything it touched — and I was not able to admit my need for Christ-like humility.

Unable to admit a need for humility — that pretty much sums up pride. I want to stop for a moment and ask, do you know this position I speak of? Being *unwilling* or *unable* to admit what you know deep down what you really need? Maybe you need help, or the humility, to apologize to someone, or to forgive another. Maybe it is time to confess something that has been a long time coming. Maybe you just know it is time to make a change. You know it deep down, but you are just not able to say the words out loud, admit your own shortcoming.

I lived this way for the longest time — unwilling to admit what I knew I needed. And I needed a lot — I needed to let go of my anger, my pride, my irritation at others, my desire to control, the list could keep going.

We can feel pride creep into our days constantly. When we don't like the way someone disagrees with us — we feel it prick. When someone says something that agitates us — it flares up. When we don't like the way we are asked to do something — we feel the jolt. When we think we are entitled to something that we are not given — that is our pride. I could go on, the list of ways that pride affects me — and likely you — is probably legitimately half a mile long. For the season in which I was going through postpartum depression, it happened to manifest itself most obviously in the form of pushing others away.

Fill in the blank, what is my area of pride?

_____

_____

_____

_____

_____

_____

_____

Where do I find myself unwilling to admit my need for change?

_____

_____

_____

Am I willing to confess today, right here on these pages, what I need to change in my life?

_____

_____

_____

What might I need to do to allow God to change me?

_____

_____

_____

—⟩|⟨—

Pushing others away became a repeated habit in my life when things got hard and I didn't want to face it — I would simply shut down. Unfortunately my personal history has shown that shutting down and pushing others out has often started with pushing away my own mom. Not only is my mom one of those closest to me in life, she is extremely wise. I can always bank on my mom having something to say that will make sense. When I am in those seasons, I often don't want to hear what makes sense, because I don't want to have to make a change.

Is there evidence of this in my life — do I push others away because what they say makes sense and I am not ready to listen?

_____

_____

_____

Who comes to mind?

_____

_____

_____

On top of wisdom, my mother is so dang stubborn. She refuses to sit by and just let me wallow! She refuses to let Satan have me and she refuses to let me sit down and lose. So when I am in a mood to stop fighting, why would I let in someone who isn't going to let me give up?

God designed the body of Christ — that is, followers of Christ — to have many people playing many parts. We were not created to walk this journey alone. God puts others in our paths — and sometimes *in our way* — to help us see our sin for what it is. Once He has our attention He will always ask us if we are willing to put it aside to become more like Jesus. Even if you don't audibly hear it (does anyone really?) you can assume God is *always* asking you if you are ready to put aside sin to become more like Jesus. Becoming more like Jesus while we walk this Earth is kind of the *whole point*. It starts with laying down our pride and asking for a change within us.

Have you ever considered that the person who is *just so annoying* in your life might actually be the exact right tool to get you to see your own sin?

Need to take a few deep breaths?

That is a truth *ain't nobody want to hear.* Can I hear an amen?!

When we are consistently agitated over a person, an idea, or an issue, it is time to bring that agitation to God and ask Him to show us *our* sin in the issue. Even if the other person is dead wrong, our agitation is a huge red flag of what's going on in our hearts.

This is one of my very least favorite things, I'll be honest. Letting God use those around me that frustrate me, to refine me and humble me is anything but pleasant. But it has also proven to be a growth opportunity 100% of the time when I bring my own pride before Him.

Is there someone in my life right now who comes to mind?

_____

_____

_____

How might God want to use them as a tool in my life to refine me?

_____

_____

_____

—⸝⸍—

Getting back to my depression, it was a time of immense pride. From the outside looking in, it probably seemed like I was in a meager and weak place. But the truth is I did not want others to have a say in my life, I did not want to listen to reason, and I did not want to be told to fight. I wanted to lie down and be left alone. That's not meager, that is stubborn pride.

My pride was completely ruining my life — even though from the outside it looked like something else completely. We cannot be fooled by what things look like from the outside; it's what is happening on the inside that reveals our heart's true condition. *"The Lord does not look at the things people look at. People look at the outward appearance, but the Lord looks at the heart."* (1 Samuel 16:7b NIV) Whatever is going on under the surface, He knows.

There I was pushing everyone away, letting pride and Satan rule me, and then something happened one day in my bedroom. My stubborn mother started yelling. She was angry and she was yelling at the enemy. She knew I was not going to fight, she could, no doubt, see it in my eyes and feel it in my midst — I had given up. There was no fight left in me, only a pitiful surrender to the darkness. So she got up in my business and started fighting *for me*.

While listening to my mother get angry on my behalf, I got angry in response. Not at the enemy. No, that would have made too much sense. I got angry at my family! I was angry they were not letting me make my own choices. I was angry they would not let me surrender, I was angry they wouldn't just leave me alone! That angry irritation was enough to spark something in me: a small flame, a feeling, a desire — *something*! For the weeks leading up to that moment, I felt little to nothing but pure despair. And something as small as irritation felt better than that!

As I was lying there in my room that day, I began fighting. Sure it was against my mom, my sister, and my husband, but in that ridiculous fighting, I felt an awakening from within. Instead of desiring to lie prostrate in surrender, I found myself wanting to *sit up* a bit. It was the smallest little change, and yet, it happened because those around me refused to sit by and let me just give up on my own life. They played their part, they rallied those around me to pray for me and they fought the enemy on my behalf. God used them to speak right into my life, even if it was in a completely unorthodox way.

Over the next few days and weeks, I no longer wanted to lay completely prostrate on the ground — physically or spiritually. I began wanting to sit up, and then stand. I found myself slowly moving to the couch, and eventually back into the real world. As I physically inched forward, I spiritually progressed. Within the month, I began to feel like myself again, I began to *feel Jesus again*!!! The darkness had been kicked to the curb (literally — thanks to my mother) and I started to see the light again.

Words cannot describe how incredible that felt — how free I was. Pride wanted to keep me down, but it was humility that let me surrender.

If we let Him, God will reveal our pride to us, humble our hearts, and help us submit to one another out of a deep respect for Christ (Ephesians 5:21). Pride told me I did not need my family to help me. It was humility that let them in.

When we allow ourselves to be humbled, we are able to repent — change our mind, turn away from our sin, and walk toward Jesus. When this happens in our lives, we get the opportunity to show others what it looks like to not only live *for* Jesus, but to die *to ourselves* for the sake of the Gospel (Galatians 2:20). If those around us are already walking with Jesus, we might encourage them in their faith walks (1 Thessalonians 5:11). But, if they are not walking with Jesus, we might actually win them over with our actions (1 Peter 3:1).

Through the process of laying down our pride in surrender and walking in Christ-like humility, we will grow more into the glorious image of Jesus. *"And the Lord—who is the Spirit—makes us more and more like him as we are changed into his glorious image."* (2 Corinthians 3:18b NLT)

We can be changed into His glorious image! That is the gift that humility offers. That is what it looks like to lay down pride and walk away from it, time and time again. It's a refining in our lives. *"Humble yourselves before the Lord, and he will lift you up."* (James 4:10 NIV)

When pride is part of the equation, it impacts our relationships with others. It causes a break in the body of believers. All the parts are intended to work together, in beautiful harmony. But when there is a break we find damage, loss, and discouragement. It's time to recognize when we are being prideful. We may not call our ways prideful, we may not even call it sin, but *we can feel what it does within us*. It becomes lodged within us and causes a blockage, breakage, or even just plain discomfort. These are things we need to pay attention to. This is the Holy Spirit speaking to us. When we feel ourselves becoming heated, when we find that we want to defend ourselves at all costs — that is our pride. When we feel unwilling to hear out another person because we are sure that they are in the wrong — that is our pride.

How well do I know that feeling?

_____

_____

_____

Which of my relationship might this be a part of?

_____

_____

_____

I challenge you, and I challenge me. We need to pay attention, call those feelings out, and lay them at the cross.

William Law says in *The Spirit of Prayer*, "The truth is this: Pride must die in you, or nothing of heaven can live in you." He goes on to say, "Don't look at pride only as an unbecoming temper, nor a humility only as a decent virtue. The one is death, and the other is life. One is all hell, and the other is all heaven."

We need to name pride for what it is. In the book *Humility: The Secret of Redemption*, Andrew Murray (emphasis added) says it so perfectly, "all lack of love; all disregard for the needs, feelings, and weakness of others; all sharp and hasty judgments and words, *so often excused under the plea of being outright and honest*; all manifestations of temper, touchiness, and irritations; all feelings of bitterness and estrangement *have their root in nothing but pride, that only seeks itself.* Will he open his eyes to see how a dark and devilish pride creeps in almost everywhere?"

How often do we ignore those inward discomforts — that deep down we know is sin within us? How often do we excuse it as something other than pride? It is time my friends that we call it what it is, be willing to lay it all down, and surrender it to Jesus. If every one of us determined to live this way within our own daily lives, our church, our body of believers, and our families, would look completely differently to the outside world. We might inspire others with our actions, even in the midst of our shortcomings. The world might be able to see Jesus within us — *even when we fail.*

Pride is going to come in. It is unlikely any of us will ever live pride-free lives. I don't want to discourage you, or delude you into believing that is an attainable goal — what colossal failures we would all feel! No, the hope is that we will get to a place in our relationship with Jesus where we are so attuned to our Holy Spirit Helper that we feel the pride *instantly* and we want nothing more than to shed it *right then*!

Humility is something that is completely counter-cultural, it is not what our world teaches us. That is why walking in humility *will* point others to Jesus. You see our pride will *always* point people away from our loving and faithful God — our pride is a turn-off. Always, to Christians and non-Christians alike! Our pride gets in the way of people seeing Jesus, it gets in the way of our body of believers operating as one, and it gets in the way of our transformation into the glorious image of Christ.

"In your relationships with one another, have the same mindset as Christ Jesus: Who, being in very nature God, did not consider equality with God something to be used to His own advantage; rather, He made himself nothing by taking the very nature of a servant, being made in human likeness. And being found in appearance as a man, He humbled himself by

becoming obedient to death— even death on a cross!" (Philippians 2:5-8 NIV)

This is where it's at. *This* is where we want to be. *This is where we need to be headed.* If we are walking with Jesus, our goals, hopes, and thoughts should always come down to laying down our pride in submission to humility.

We can ask ourselves:

> *Am I walking in humility like Jesus did?*
> *Am I willing to name my pride and lay it down?*
> *Am I laying down my own desires in surrender of God's will?*

All of it — the good, the bad, and the dangerously ugly — it can all lead us toward His perfect presence. Humility is a Holy act of worship. Because of Who God is, we can know that He is worthy of our humility. We can believe that His will is always better than our own, and we can trust that even when we don't understand the hardships — *He is enough.*

When we surrender to our Lord, we will experience more of His presence.

When we surrender to our Lord, we can experience harmony within the body of Christ, and trust that our individual roles are designed and purposed to benefit the family of believers as a whole.

When we surrender to our Lord, we can trust we are walking in His will.

What do I need to surrender in humility to experience more of His presence?

_____

_____

_____

Chapter Eighteen

IN THE WORDS OF MY AUNT:
IT ALL BOILS DOWN TO TRUST.

It all boils down to trust. Do I trust Him?

Period.

Season after season of dark and confusing times has lead me to this exact question: *Do I trust Him?*

Either I do, or I don't.

Years ago I defined trust as a personal belief in something to come, without a lot of God in the equation. I think many of us fall into the trap of removing God from our "faith equation". Today I would redefine trust as this: the belief that God is good, and that is enough. Whatever He determines for my life is best — whether I like it or not — He knows what is best, He has our best interest in mind, and that is enough for me.

Do I trust Him?

Either I do, or I don't.

Have you ever evaluated your faith or circumstances in such uncomplicated terms? It's pretty fantastically simple when it is all boiled down.

We don't have to like our circumstances, but we do have to decide if we will trust God or not.

Jesus didn't want to die on the cross, He didn't want to suffer and be tortured, He didn't want to experience the weight of our world's punishment. We know this because He asked God to take the burden from Him. We know this because it is recorded in the gospels:

"'My soul is very sorrowful, even to death; remain here, and watch with Me.' And going a little farther He fell on His face and prayed, saying, 'My Father, if it be possible, let this cup pass from Me'". Matthew 26:38-39a

Let this cup pass from Me. That is what Jesus asked God before He was to be tortured and murdered.

How much more relatable could our Savior be?! He did not choose to walk a painful path. It was not His choice to endure hardships, He *wanted* to be excused from them in this life if possible. Yet, He surrendered in perfect obedience to the will of the Father. Raise your hand if that brings you some comfort: *even Jesus* would take a pass on hardships too.

Wishing for a pass doesn't make us failures, or unfaithful. It makes us human.

Where we go from that desire is another thing. The other half of the verse is so beautiful! Read it with me: *"Father, if it be possible, let this cup pass from Me; **nevertheless, not as I will, but as You will.**"* (Matthew 26:39; emphasis added)

Jesus had all the same human desires we have, to skip the hard stuff. Yet, when it came right down to it — He really only wanted God's will for His life.

He trusted the Father.

We either trust the Father, or we don't.

Not a single trial I walked through was enjoyable to me. Not a single hardship we'll go through is likely to be pleasant. And yet we can still choose the will of the Father first.

I don't like it, I don't want it, but I want your will more, Lord.

Either I trust God, or I don't.

How does that simplistic approach to my faith change things for me?

_____

_____

_____

_____

_____

What, if any, convictions does it bring to my heart?

_____

_____

_____

_____

_____

How might it bring freedom?

_____

_____

_____

_____

Each and every thing we walk through in this life brings us closer to Jesus, or takes us further away. There is no in-between. The in-between is called *lukewarm faith*, which is repulsive to God. In each and every circumstance we must choose which direction we will head. Starting by asking ourselves the simple question: *do I trust Him?*

A man named Greg Morse wrote an article for desiringgod.org about the recognition of his own lukewarm faith. He says, "I convinced myself that I was safe from the wrath of God. No one told me that the lukewarm 'Christian' gets spit out of God's mouth (Revelation 3:16). No one informed me that if God was not first in my heart, I was either in urgent need of repentance, or I was lost. In the words of Francis Chan, 'I was lukewarm and lovin' it.'"

Friends, there is no in-between. Upstream or down. You don't stay stagnant in a river, and you don't in faith.

You grow closer or further.

I started this book by admitting some depression creeping back into my life. It wasn't circumstantial — it was spiritual. I hated it, it is such an awful experience. Yet, I had a choice: pull the covers over my eyes and lie down in defeat, or open up the Word and get busy fighting — get busy trusting. One choice would pull me downstream, and one would pull me up. Neither would leave me sitting comfortably in the same place.

It's been four months since I typed that first line, and that darkness hasn't left me completely. It lingers, but it does not consume — a victory in my book! I firmly believe God has used the writing of this book to pull me ever so gently away from the pit I had previously embraced during those postpartum days. I felt Him press on me the need to start writing, and while I wanted to say *no*, I trusted Him more. So I started writing, and would you look at that, I've written a book.

When I felt consumed with darkness, God reminded me that *Jesus is the light*. His Word is the light, and in Him I can safely rest even when all else is muddled and confusing.

This book has been a saving grace in my life through another dark season. A different type of dark season, but a dark one nonetheless. They won't stop coming, these types of seasons. Until the day that we die we will experience hard things in this life that we won't want to walk through. But friends, for every dark season, there is Jesus, and in Jesus there is light.

I pray you are encouraged by this book, because I know I have been. The time spent in the word throughout these pages, and the prayers invested on both your behalf and mine, God has used to remind me that *I already know* exactly how to fight in these seasons.

Do I trust him?

"*Not my will, Lord, but yours be done.*" (Luke 22:42b NIV)

Press in, trust the Father, and *know* that we will continue to be transformed more and more into the glorious image of Jesus.

_____

_____

_____

_____

Acknowledgments

A FEW SHOUT OUTS

First and foremost — I want to thank my God. Lord, without Your prompting, and dare-I-say, insistence, I never would have written this book. Yet, beyond that, I thank You for knowing what I need and how I need it. Thank You for taking me on wild rides that I would never have signed up for. Thank You for showing me so gently and mercifully the error of my ways, always steering me back to Your path. Thank You for the gift of hindsight, where so many things are learned in my life. Thank You for being You, and allowing me to love and serve You.

To my husband, Joey — thank you for being my partner in life. You came along on all these journeys with me, and you lovingly support me no matter what I need. You rarely ask for anything in return, and you love me even when I am unlovable. Thank you for your unending support in this life and during this book writing process.

To my children — I adore you, each of you: Randy, Michael, Amber, David, Brighton, Aida, Ephraim and Elend. Not all of your stories made it in this book, but I cherish each of you. The ways God lead each of you to us leaves me daily with an equally, amazing, wonderment of God's goodness. Thank you for letting me be your mom. I pray you know how thankful I am for that role in your life.

To my mom — you have been such a consistent fighter in my life. You fight for me, for my transformation, against the enemy, against my pride, and my flesh. God has consistently used you to help me see the need to lay down my sin and seek Jesus. Thank you for never backing down when I have pushed you away and challenged you. Thank you for your love and encouragement in everything I do. I know you believe in me, and you have no idea how much that means to me.

To my sister, Melissa — thank you for your support in everything I do. You had every right to walk away from me forever, but you never gave up on me. You always believed Jesus could change me, and shape me into the sister you deserved (my words, not yours!). Thank you for reading this book and getting excited for me, cheering me on, and most of all offering your incredible insight into what would make this book better for my readers.

To my dad — your constant work on my book brings a smile to my face, and a swell in my heart. I loved hopping on to google docs and seeing you actively working late in the night. You challenged me, encouraged me, and helped me to clean up this book. Thank you for helping me rewrite nearly ALL the questions in a way that would provoke insightful, thoughtful, reflections from my readers. Thank you for your support and love throughout this book and in my life, you have no idea what it means to me.

To my friend Glenda — you will never understand the impact you have had on my life. I don't know what I would do without your friendship. You are one of my favorite people in this world, and I have seen your love for Jesus radiate from the moment I met you, all those years ago. Thank you for your help and encouragement with this book. Thank you for all the personal little touches you have added, and your constant joy for me in the process!

To my Aunt Liz — thank you for being my challenger. Thank you for believing in me, and yet knowing that there is always work for Jesus to do in me. Thank you for asking me the hard questions, and sharing from your personal life. Lastly, thank you for reading my book and offering your insight and support!

To my ministry partner and friend Hannah — this book most likely wouldn't exist without you! God spoke this ministry into existence through your idea and dream, and because of this ministry, I believe God lead me to this book. Thank you for your friendship, love, and support, in this book and in life!

To my test readers — Kristin, Pastor James, Holly, Meghan, Liz, Glenda, Joey, Melissa, Mom, Dad, Hannah: This book wouldn't be what it has become without you. I truly and completely appreciate every single thought you poured into it. You took the time to read it not only for yourself, but also imagining the perspective that other readers would see things and helping me to reshape things. Thank you so much for your insight, help and support.

Made in the
USA
Columbia, SC